*The Blue Guide to
the Here and Hereafter*

THE BLUE GUIDE TO THE HERE AND HEREAFTER

*Lionel Blue and
Jonathan Magonet*

COLLINS
8 Grafton Street, London W1
1988

William Collins Sons & Co Ltd
London · Glasgow · Sydney · Auckland
Toronto · Johannesburg

BRITISH LIBRARY CATALOGUING IN PUBLICATION DATA

Blue, Lionel
The blue guide to the here and
hereafter.
1. Jewish way of life
I. Title   II. Magonet, Jonathan
296.7'4   BM723

ISBN 0-00-217714-5

First published 1988
Reprinted 1988
Second reprint 1988
© Lionel Blue and Jonathan Magonet 1988

Set in Linotype Palatino by
Rowland Phototypesetting,
Bury St Edmunds, Suffolk
Made and printed in Great Britain by
T.J. Press (Padstow) Ltd, Padstow, Cornwall

CONTENTS

Prologue   13

A DAY

1   MORNING   19

Waking up in the morning   19
Morning blues   19
The loo – privy thoughts   20
The bathroom – cleanliness and Godliness   20
My body   21
Getting dressed   22
The news   23
Turning on the radio and TV – the celebrity   25
The message in the media   26
The silent room   27
The importance of wearing a hat   29
High heels   30
A button   30
Leaving the house and seeing a rainbow   31
Waiting in the station   32
Seeing people off   33
Food for the journey – will there be a buffet?   34

2   BUSINESS OF LIFE   36

Signing our name on cheques and on our lives   36
Making a living   37
Business people   38
Market traders   39
Wages   40
Paying the bill   42
In debt   43
Taxes   43

Committees   44
Politics   45
Rows   46

3 GOING HOME   48

In the supermarket   48
Doctors   49
Waiting rooms   51
Waiting room wisdom   52
Tired and fed up on a suburban train   53
Delays, breakdowns and industrial disputes   55
Returning home   58
A bench in the park   60
Goodlooking people   61
Meeting a beggar   63
Living with lodgers   64
Suburban dreams   65
The eye is not satisfied with seeing   66
Housework   67
Teatime chitchat   69
Gardening   70
Pious potatoes   71
"Taste and see that the Lord is good"   74
Kitchen logic   75
Cocktail party thoughts   75
Dinner party   76
Dining in heaven or hell   77
Card games   78
Reading books   79
Writing books   80
Lullabies   80
Going to bed   81

A LIFE

4 LIVING   85

This is your life   85
What is this life?   86
Growing up   87
Dilemmas of daily life and problems posed
    by Scripture   89

Questioned by life 90
Living with handicaps 90
Prejudice 91
Scapegoats 92
Passing the buck 93
Taking responsibility 95
Promises, promises! 96

5 LOVE 97

Confirmation in the back row of the cinema 97
Being stood up 98
Boy loses girl 101
True love 102
Expressions of love 102
Love of a husband for his wife 106
Love of a wife for her husband 107
Illusions of love 108
Memories of love 110

6 RELATIONSHIPS 113

Animals – calves, asses and small creatures 113
Mothers in sentiment, spirit and sociology 115
When your husband walks out on you 116
A father fighting to keep his pride 117
Children 118
When the kids were young 119

7 CHALLENGES 121

Breakdown 121
Facing the music 122
Courage 122
Middle age 123
Midlife crisis 125
Living with oneself 126
Nostalgia 127
Suicidal 128
When Hell happens 129
Exile 133
The price of survival 134

Taking stock – sorting out the debris in
  drawers and in us 134
Hanging on 136

8 PROSPECTS 138

Old Age – "The evil days?" 138
Illness 140
Making a will 141
In the hospital 142
Terminal illness 146
Dying 147
The cemetery – the "house of life" 150
Mourning 151
The last judgement 152
Our eternal home 153

ETERNITY

9 THE RIDDLE 157

Riddle of life 157
Why me? 158
It's not fair! 159
Life is tough 161
It is ordained 162
Self-fulfilling hypotheses and pseudo-events 164
False charity 166
True charity 167
Trying to understand our nationalism 169

10 THE RELIGIOUS QUEST 171

Hunting for God 171
Searching for God 173
Meeting God 174
Losing faith 175
Places of worship 176
Clergy 177
Cutting the cackle 177
Hide and seek 178
God's address 179
True and false Gods 179
Teachers 180

CONTENTS

Saviours 183
Messiahs 183
Thirty-six righteous people 185
Cautions about religion 186
Questions about religion 187
Pious fools 188
Checklist 189
Arguing with God 190
Arguing with tradition 191
Arguing with ourselves 193
To yourself be true 194
The importance of atheists 196
Returning 196
Religion and magic 198
Resignation 199
Without the mystery what's left? 200
Seeing stars 200

11 ALL HAVING BEEN SAID 205

Graffiti 205
Wise sayings we don't understand 205

Epilogue 206
Who's Who 208
What's What 218
Acknowledgements 222

God full of compassion, grant perfect rest beneath the
shelter of Your presence among the holy and pure
who shine as the lights of heaven to our teachers

Anneliese Debray
Tony Garcia
Joanna Mary Hughes
Dr Charlotte Klein
Dr Ellen Littmann
Michael Maybaum
Rav Shmuel Sperber
Rabbi Dr Werner Van der Zyl

PROLOGUE

Many books on spirituality

I enjoy books on spirituality, but I am wary of them, because I can't recognize myself and my situation in them. They start off from where I ought to be, not from where I am, and are as aggravating as British road signs, because they don't tell me how I get from where I am to where I ought to be.

I hope this book starts off where you are – on your knees (if you are praying or plastered), or prostrate (before an ark or altar or in bed), or in a bar, bistro, bath or bus queue. The situations are set out in sequence because they mark the changes in our days and lives. Prayerbooks mark the seasons, with hymns for harvests and sowing and such. For people who harvest their frozen food in supermarkets, this is pious poetry, not the practical round of their daily life. In this anthology, there is much poetry, because it illuminates life's prose as well as its loveliness.

The extracts are all written by Jews, generously defined, but their use is general. Jews are useful because they are ordinary human beings, only more so, and where there are two Jews there are three opinions. They thus provide a précis of the human condition, and if you can put aside your prejudices, you too can locate yourself in the religious rugger scrum of Jewish life, whatever your birth or background.

Now Jewish tradition may not always reach the heights of a St John of the Cross or the depths of a Kierkegaard, but it is much more normal and a lot less miserable. It also starts off from people's religious needs in this world, not God's glory in the next.

Judaism is also not the religion of a church or sect but of an entire people who are bound together more by history and experience than by belief, so the writers are of all classes and conditions and confessions. Some confess the God of tradition, some confess they can't find Him. It doesn't matter. The truth speaks through them too. Another Jew once said, "By their fruits ye shall know them", and though this is not read in synagogues, it is a good test.

The forms in which these truths are revealed are many and various – the only barrier against many of the extracts is unfamiliarity which is a cause of religious prejudice. They did not first appear as plump, self-important scriptures, but as graffiti on cellar walls, and poems and letters of ordinary couples caught up in the whirlwind of terrifying times. The truth proceeds from tin pan alley, as well as from concentration camps, for many Jewish voices come out of a juke box. God, unlike His followers, uses everything that serves, and is no spiritual snob.

Rabbi Magonet and I are two pillars of a Reform Jewish establishment. He is the head of its seminary, and I am concerned with canon law and convene its courts. He seems the more venerable, for he sports a beard – though "sports" is too frivolous a word for so grave a growth.

But we were not always so grave. Rabbi Dr Magonet once strummed a guitar and accompanied his own songs on it in continental cafés (they were more cheerful than the songs of Zion), while I danced in discos.

All aspects of our lives have gone to make up this anthology. We have tried to be marriage brokers, joining the natural to the supernatural and bringing a particular and practical tradition of spirituality and sense, to the universal problems and passions of ordinary people everywhere.

The nature and form of Jewish literature are daunting, for commentary piles up on commentary, and few know their way through such a jungle. Four languages are essential for the search: Hebrew, Aramaic, Yiddish and Ladino. Of these the second is dead, and the last two may be dying. But even these would need Russian, Polish, German, Arabic and English at least as supplements. But this anthology may spur on some courageous readers to hack out a path for themselves. In the topsy-turvy history of the Jews, there is something for readers of all religions and none.

A religion, like a human being, does not exist for itself but for others. For its own sake it has to play its part in the cosmic chain – giving and receiving, constantly discarding beloved debris, and assimilating fresh truth. The alternative is atrophy and death. Too many religions have become self-admiration societies or exclusive clubs. Self-centred religions wither like self-centred people. If this Jewish anthology illuminates a human life, it has served its purpose – a human being trying to heave her- or himself out of bed on a bleak winter morning; or someone praying to an unknown power in a Harley Street waiting room, or a lover and his lass dancing in a disco. Are they Jewish? I don't know, and it doesn't matter.

All of us have inherited the Holocaust. It is like a lump which we still carry on our back, and until the end of this century certainly, one generation will pass it on to the other. Before we can exorcize it, we have to peer into its blackness and begin to understand it. It is our dark night, more actual than any literary one, and it is not only in history, it is inside us too, like a cancer. We have tried to let many ghostly voices from the past speak in these pages, because their goodness dissipates some of the terror. Though we cannot locate God in the holocaust, through such witnesses at least we know He was not absent – and that brings some relief. Finding God in the history of the holocaust will help us come across Him in our private hells and holocausts. A religiosity which does not address itself to such tasks is slop!

Some of the passages may not seem divine or devotional, but the kingdom of heaven is within you as well as outside you or beyond you, so you cannot know God without trying to know yourself or your situation. If you try for the former without the latter, the Almighty will get lost in an almighty muddle of evasion. In our situation the divine cannot be known directly, only through human voices, ideas and mental images. We hope you will see the divinity in the humanity of these extracts.

Interspersed among them are our own comments. They are there to pinpoint the relevance of the unfamiliar and to help you relate to a tradition which has its own in-language and terms. For this reason a What's What and a Who's Who have been added at the end. The choice of extracts has not been determined by their grandeur or fame, but because they have touched us, the editors, and they might touch your life too.

The book was composed in this way. Sarah Baird-Smith of Collins asked me what book I wanted to work on. I thought about it, and told her: a book which brings together all the strands of

Jewish spirituality – authorized and unauthorized, pious and comic – and then releases them from their ghetto to be of use to people of all faiths and none, in the doubts and dilemmas of their daily life and work.

I then approached Jonathan Magonet and asked him whether we could work on it together, because, as I have said, he is a friend, a colleague and above all a scholar with imagination and vision. We had already worked together for many years, editing and composing liturgy and relating it to life.

Jonathan was mainly responsible for discovering texts, and I was mainly responsible for comments. We are both responsible for the serious, comic and singular result.

As you read it we wish you Mazel Tov! – Good Luck! And God go with you.

LIONEL BLUE

A Day

The day is short, and the work is great,
and the labourers are sluggish,
and the wages are high,
and the Master of the house is insistent.

Sayings of the Fathers 2:20

1 · MORNING

Waking up in the morning

A rehearsal of the resurrection

When you wake up you put in some practice for your own resurrection.

Blessed are You, Lord our God, king of the universe, who takes away sleep from my eyes and slumber from my eyelids.

Siddur

My God, the soul You have given me is pure, for You created it, You formed it and You made it live within me. You watch over it within me, but one day You will take it from me to everlasting life. My God and God of my fathers, as long as the soul is within me, I will declare that You are the master of all deeds, the ruler of all creatures and the Lord of every soul. Blessed are You Lord, who brings the dead into everlasting life.

Siddur

Morning blues

Man is afraid of things that cannot harm him, and he knows it. And he longs for things that cannot help him, and he knows it. But actually it is something within man that he is afraid of, and it is something within man that he longs for.

Chasidic

To worry is a sin. Only one sort of worry is permissible: to worry because one worries.

RABBI NOAH LEKHIVITZER

Someone else's worries do not take away your sleep.

YIDDISH PROVERB

The loo – privy thoughts

At the home of a holy woman, they said her house was exactly as she had left it, which was not accurate, as they had pulled down her privy.

Blessing to be recited on relieving oneself in the morning

Blessed are You, Lord our God, king of the universe, who fashioned the human body with wisdom and created within it many openings and many cavities. It is obvious and known before Your Throne of Glory that if one of them was opened or one of them was blocked it would be impossible to survive and stand before You. Blessed are You Lord, who heals all flesh and acts in wondrous ways.

Siddur

In the privy it is prohibited to think of matters of the Torah; it is therefore best to concentrate his thoughts upon his business and accounts while there, in order that he might not come to think of matters of the Torah or, God forbid, to think of some violation of the law. On the Sabbath, when it is not permitted to think about business, he should think of some wonderful things that he had either seen or heard, or the like.

Kitzur Shulchan Aruch 4:4

The bathroom – cleanliness and Godliness

A bath is the origin of baptism and can also make you feel a new person though it is too humble to be considered holy.

Wash me free from my guilt
and cleanse me from my sin.

Psalm 51:4

Once when Hillel left his disciples, they said to him, "Where are you going?" He replied, "To do a pious deed." They said, "What may that be?" He said, "To take a bath." They asked, "Is that a pious deed?" He answered, "Yes, for if the man who is appointed to tend and wash the images of kings which are set up in the theatres and circuses, receives his rations for so doing, and is even raised up to be regarded as among the great ones of the kingdom, how much more is it obligatory on me to tend and wash my body, since I have been created in the image of God."

Leviticus Rabbah 34:3

My body

God speaks through your body as well as through your brain and soul. Its reactions are more honest, because it does not have their subtlety to cheat.

There are six parts of the body that serve a person; three are under his control and three are not under his control.

The eye, the ear, and the nose are not under a person's control: he sees what he doesn't want to see, hears what he doesn't want to hear, and smells what he doesn't want to smell.

The mouth, the hand, and the foot are under a person's control; if he wants, he can use his mouth to study Torah, or if he wants he can use it to speak gossip and blasphemy; if he wishes, he can use his hand to distribute charity, or if he wishes, he can use it to steal and kill; if he chooses to, he can use his feet to walk to synagogues or houses of study, or if he chooses to, he can walk to houses of bawdy entertainment or immorality.

Genesis Rabbah 67:3

Anyway, can I pretend I have much choice? I look at myself and see chest, thighs, feet – a head. This strange organization, I know it will die. And inside – something, something, happiness . . . "Thou movest me." That leaves no choice. Something produces intensity, a holy feeling, as oranges produce orange, as grass green, as birds heat. Some hearts put out more love and some less of it, presumably. Does it signify anything? There are those who say this product of hearts is knowledge . . . I couldn't say that, for sure. My face too blind, my mind too limited, my instincts too narrow. But this intensity, doesn't it mean anything? Is it an idiot joy that makes this animal, the most peculiar animal of all, exclaim something? And he thinks this reaction a sign, a proof, of eternity? And he has it in his breast? But I have no arguments to make about it. "Thou movest me." "But what do you want . . . ?" "But that's just it – not a solitary thing. I am pretty well satisfied to be, to be just as it is willed, and for as long as I may remain in occupancy."

SAUL BELLOW

Getting dressed

Knots and tassels in our handkerchiefs or clothing tie our conscience to this world, and this world to the next in our mind and memory. Knotty and neurotic problems arise if you overdo this pious desire.

The Lord said to Moses: "Speak to the children of Israel and tell them that each generation shall put tassels on the corner of their clothes, and put a blue thread on the corner tassel. When this tassel catches your eye, you will remember all the Lord's commands and do them. Then you will no longer wander after the desires of your heart and your eyes which led you to lust. Then you will remember all My commands and do them and you will be set apart for your God. I am the Lord your God, who brought you out of the land of Egypt, to be your own God. I, the Lord, am your God."

Numbers 15:37–41

I prepare to wrap myself in this *Tallit* (prayer shawl) to fulfil the command of my creator. As it is written in the Torah: "Each generation shall put tassels on the corners of their clothes." And just as I cover myself with a robe in this world, so may my soul deserve to be clothed in a beautiful robe in the world to come, as in Eden.

Siddur

The word "tassels" can also be translated as "fringes" or "knots". It is said that Baden Powell, a devoted Bible reader, invented the Boy Scout's "toggle" through reading this passage.

Once a king had a terrifying dream which he told to his vizier. He dreamt that the wheat that would grow the following year would drive anyone who ate it mad. So they discussed how to deal with this threat. The vizier suggested: "Let us store up some normal wheat for ourselves this year and we can live off it in the following year when everyone else eats the bad wheat and becomes crazy." But the king pointed out that if they alone were sane while everyone else was mad, the others would think them mad and kill them. Finally the king found a solution: "Let us also eat the wheat and become mad like the others. But before we eat it, we will each make a knot in our belt. Then whenever we gaze upon the knot in the future, at least we will know that we are mad."

Based on NACHMAN of Bratslav

One should be very careful not to put on two garments at the same time, because this is harmful to one's memory!

Kitzur Shulchan Aruch

The news

So often it's sad stuff, but you can't dive back under your duvet! The world is a tricky place. Can you tell the difference between the tinned milk of human kindness and the fresh product? It's not easy when the medium has become the message, and the packaging has improved so much.

They say: "Peace!" "Peace!" but there is no peace.

Jeremiah 6:14

Many simple people ask you: "Do you think the war will be over soon?" And if you innocently answer: "Yes, very soon", you suddenly notice – and at first, you refuse to believe it – fear and dismay spreading over their faces. They are slightly embarrassed at this and at least know that they ought to be glad for humane reasons. But the war has brought them bread and a good income, for some the first time in their lives, for others the first time in years, and so one single feeling torments them: If only it goes on for a while, if only it doesn't end that soon! Whole nations, down to the lowest strata, have become war-profiteers, with all the concomitant reactions to the world. If I were to express the thing that has filled me with the most despair during this war, it would be this daily experience: the war as a breadwinner and as security.

ELIAS CANETTI

In the last century, man suffered from a lack of knowledge; in our time, man suffers from too much knowledge, from intentionally produced false knowledge. And if our intellect is insufficient or misdirected, this also applies to our feelings. All of us know this. The death of an infant moves us; the death of six million people simply stuns our senses.

We are Eichmann's sons, removed from the consequences of our actions. The fine edge of our sensibilities has been worn away by the monstrosities of our age. The six o'clock news is the most brutal programme on television – and we do not even turn it off. Each day, murder and destruction flicker across the screen as part of our home life. Is it any wonder that we have learned to live comfortably with the knowledge of the death of the six million? We can keep a body count of our own, right in the privacy of our livingroom.

ALBERT H. FRIEDLANDER

This encourages me in my layman's view that the importance of the prophets, both for their generation and for us, is not that they speak "comfortable words" (though they do that too at times), but that they dare to say things which are very uncomfortable indeed but which happen to be true. Their interest was not in morale (so-called) but in something very different: morals. . . .

The methods of the old false prophet were the same as those of the new: the manipulation of fact, the histrionic use of language, the endless self-praise, the merciless repetitions: "The Temple of the Lord, the Temple of the Lord, the Temple of the Lord are these." Modern science has only refined these old weapons. It conditions and reconditions men to buy goods they do not need and to worship leaders who enslave them.

LEON ROTH

When Hillel saw a skull floating on the surface of the water, he said, Because you drowned others, they drowned you, and in the end those who drowned you shall themselves be drowned.

Sayings of the Fathers 2:7

Turning on the radio and TV – the celebrity

The radio, the TV, and the morning papers. As the day begins, we are quickly sucked into the real world of fantasy. We say it is "real" because it is made up of our own reflections.

An important problem in morning prayer is to sort out what is real and what is reflection before we get too involved and can't tell the difference.

The celebrity in the distinctive modern sense could not have existed in any earlier age, or in America before the Graphic Revolution. *The celebrity is a person who is known for his well-knownness.*

His qualities – or rather his lack of qualities – illustrate our peculiar problems. He is neither good nor bad, great nor petty. He is the human pseudo-event. He has been fabricated on purpose to satisfy our exaggerated expectations of human greatness. He is morally neutral. The product of no conspiracy, of no group promoting vice or emptiness, he is made by honest, industrious men of high professional ethics doing their job, "informing" and educating us. He is made by all of us who willingly read about him, who like to see him on television, who buy recordings of his voice, and talk about him to our friends. His relation to morality and even to reality is highly ambiguous. He is like the woman in an Elinor Glyn novel who describes another by saying "she is like a figure in an Elinor Glyn novel".

DANIEL J. BOORSTIN

**All there is to know about
Adolph Eichmann**

Eyes:	*Medium*
Hair:	*Medium*
Weight:	*Medium*

Height:	*Medium*
Distinguishing features:	*None*
Number of fingers:	*Ten*
Number of toes:	*Ten*
Intelligence:	*Medium*
What did you expect?	
Talons?	
Oversize incisors?	
Green saliva?	
Madness?	

LEONARD COHEN

The message in the media

"The eye is not satisfied with seeing nor the ear with hearing", for though the things of this world such as people and objects can be ways to what we want, they are not really what we want. Our soul is not satisfied by them.

Not long ago I met a public relations adviser who held a responsible position in a large and influential firm. His specialty was writing – speeches, articles, letters – for public figures. I asked him how much he consulted with his clients. He explained that of course he had to meet and know the men for whom he wrote, in order to be able to write like them. But, he said, a difficulty in working for the same clients over an extended period was that, if you were successful in writing for them, it became harder and harder to know what they were really like. His clients, he said, had an incurable tendency to forget that they had not written their own speeches. When he asked them in briefing sessions what they thought of this or that, they were increasingly inclined to quote to the public relations adviser the very speech which the counsel had supplied them a few weeks before. It was disturbing, he said, to hear yourself quoted to yourself by somebody else who thought it was himself speaking: you began to wonder whether it was your language after all.

This suggested to my public relations adviser friend another example of the same problem. A client had decided to move his plant away, and therefore to change his public relations adviser to a firm in the city where his new plant would be located. This client telephoned my friend, explained the situation, and asked him to ghost-write a letter to be sent to the head of the public relations firm, explaining the situation, enumerating his regrets, and generally keeping up the image which the firm had helped him build up over the years. My friend wrote the letter. A few days later the head of the public relations firm called in my ghost-writing friend, told him he had a piece of bad news, namely, that Mr X was moving his firm away and would have to drop their services. But, the boss said, there were only the warmest feelings (as he had just learned from the letter he had received); now he wanted my friend to draft a nice letter which he as head of the firm could send, explaining *his* regrets that the business connection was being terminated. My friend remarked that he was probably the highest-paid man ever employed to write letters to himself.

DANIEL J. BOORSTIN

The impulse to evil is like one who runs about the world keeping his hand closed. Nobody knows what he has inside of it. He goes up to everyone and asks: "What do you suppose I have in my hand?" And every person thinks that just what he wants most of all is hidden there. And everyone runs after the impulse to evil. Then he opens his hand and it is empty.

Chasidic

The silent room

Words are not the main way to God, nor is noise, whether ecclesiastical or otherwise. People often multiply their prayers, to prevent God getting a word in edgeways. The silence is not a nothing or an absence. It vibrates, as you can find out for yourself, if you are willing to experience it. Fifteen minutes is usually enough.

And, behold, the Lord passed by, and a great and strong wind rent the mountains, and broke in pieces the rocks before the Lord; but the Lord was not in the wind; and after the wind an earthquake; but the Lord was not in the earthquake; and after the earthquake a fire; but the Lord was not in the fire; and after the fire the voice of thin silence.

1 Kings 19:11–12

It is good to steady yourself with silence. Eternity is all round you and is friendlier than you think. But you have to shut out the background noise outside you and inside you. Silence is not something to frighten' you.

> You do not have to leave the room.
> Remain standing at your table and listen.
> Do not even listen, simply wait.
> Do not even wait.
> Be quite still and solitary.
>
> The world will freely offer itself to you.
> To be unmasked.
> It has no choice.
> It will roll in ecstasy at your feet.

FRANZ KAFKA

The environment which I feel to be the natural one, the situation which has been assigned to me as my fate, the things that happen to me day after day, the things that claim me day after day – these contain my essential task and such fulfilment of existence as is open to me . . . The Baal Shem teaches that no encounter with a being or a thing in the course of our life lacks a hidden significance. The people we live with or meet with, the animals that help us with our farmwork, the soil we till, the materials we shape, the tools we use, they all contain a mysterious spiritual substance which depends on us for helping it towards its pure form, its perfection. If we neglect this spiritual substance sent across our path, if we think only in terms of momentary purposes, without developing a genuine relationship to the beings and things in whose life we ought to take part, as they in ours, then we shall ourselves be debarred from true fulfilled existence.

MARTIN BUBER

Rabbi Moshe Leib said:
"A human being who has not a single hour for his own every day is no human being."

MARTIN BUBER

The importance of wearing a hat

Putting on your hat

According to Lytton Strachey, Cardinal Manning laboured all his life to acquire his hat and it crowned his tomb. The same superfluous article is a problem for Jews too. Traditional Jews wear one when they pray. Some Progressive Jews prefer not. This is a cause of controversy!

On 10th November 1938, the Nazis celebrated what in their never-never language they called Crystal Night. During the black hours of that night, they burned or demolished stone by stone every Synagogue in Germany. A week or so later we at (Temple) Beth El decided to have a service of grief and sorrow for the Synagogues that were destroyed. To the special service we invited all Jewish refugees in Providence (Rhode Island). On that Friday night, about ten minutes before the service was to begin, a man then active in the congregation rushed into the little room at the rear of the Temple where I sat: "Did you give permission to these people to wear hats?" The fact was that until that instant I had given no thought to the headgear of our guests – the refugees. I did not know whether or not our guests chose to wear hats, to put on *Yarmulkes*, or not to wear either. And so my response to the question which sounded to me like "When did you stop beating your Mother?" was indirect. I began to say: "But these people are our guests. They have suffered so much. Whether or not they choose to wear their hats, surely we do not wish to add insult to the injuries they have already suffered." But my interrogator was implacable. "Answer my question. Did you or did you not give permission to these people to wear their hats?" To this day, I don't know the outcome of the battle of the hats. I was too choked up with pain. Involuntarily I thought of comparable demands – of Cossack officers saying to Jews "*Shapka doloi*", "Off with your hat", of SS men saying, "*Hut ab, Jude*". So when I walked into the Temple I did not look. My head was reeling; my eyes were filled with tears. To this day I do not know whether ushers took it upon themselves to tell our guests to remove their hats and whether some of the refugees left in protest. Whatever happened to the hats worn by our guests, that service for me at least was indeed a service of grief and sorrow.

WILLIAM G. BRAUDE

High heels

God help me!
My head, I carry my head so high
no one I love can reach me.

God help me!
Wherever I go I see my slaves plodding
my loads laid on their bent necks,
my hand goes out to them, and I run after
   them
with my head up, on high heels.

God help me!
When I, I myself am so pale so thin
a little bread's enough for me and
a couple of yards would do
to wrap up this body –
why are so many backs
bowed beneath my loads?

Ah God, help my haughty head, and my
   high heels.

MALKA HEIFETZ TUSSMAN

A button

A Button

The button thinks –
Take it all in all,
Nobody finds life easy.
You live alone,

Or you are attached.
Alone life is sad,
But the constant round is tedious.
I would rather be sad.
Yet I haven't the courage to break away.
I'll try again.

A. LUTZKY

Leaving the house and seeing a rainbow

And God said to Noah: "I set My bow in the cloud and it shall be a sign of the covenant between Me and the earth. When I bring clouds over the earth and the bow is seen in the clouds I will remember My covenant which is between Me and you and every living creature of all flesh, and the waters shall never again become a flood to destroy all flesh."

Genesis 9:13–15

On seeing a rainbow one recites the blessing: Blessed are You, Lord our God, king of the universe, who remembers His covenant and is faithful to it, and keeps His promise.

Siddur

What is the rainbow? It is God's bow turned upside down so the arrows shoot away from the earth and bring no more destruction.

Jewish legend

Somewhere Over the Rainbow

When all the world is a hopeless jumble
And the raindrops tumble all around
Heaven opens a magic lane.

When all the clouds darken up the skyway
There's a rainbow highway to be found
Leaving from your window pane
To a place behind the sun
Just a step beyond the rain.

Somewhere over the rainbow
Way up high
There's a land that I heard of
Once in a lullaby.
Somewhere over the rainbow
Skies are blue
And the dreams that you dare to dream
Really do come true.

Some day I'll wish upon a star
And wake up where the clouds are far behind me.
Where troubles melt like lemon drops,
Away above the chimney tops
That's where you'll find me.

Somewhere over the rainbow
Bluebirds fly
Birds fly over the rainbow
Why then, oh why can't I?
If happy little bluebirds fly
Beyond the rainbow
Why oh why can't I?

E. Y. HARBURG

Waiting in the station

A meditation on the way to work.

"You can learn something from everything", the rabbi of Sada-
gora once said to his hasidim. "Everything can teach us some-
thing, and not only everything God has created. What man has
made has also something to teach us."
"What can we learn from a train?" one hasid asked dubiously.
"That because of one second one can miss everything."
"And from the telegraph?"
"That every word is counted and charged."
"And the telephone?"
"That what we say here is heard there."

MARTIN BUBER

Seeing people off

You see poor people waving and crying on the platform. They speak strange languages, they block your way and you get annoyed because they are a nuisance. But you have to see them as they see themselves, and, even more important, as God sees them.

In the evening when we were alone together my mother would make me sit on her footstool, and while her deft fingers manipulated the knitting needles she would gaze into my eyes as if she tried to absorb enough of me to last her for the coming months of absence. "You will write us, dear?" she kept asking continually. "And if I should die when you are gone, you will remember me in your prayers." . . .

At the moment of departure (from Eastern Europe to America), when the train drew into the station, she lost control of her feelings. As she embraced me for the last time her sobs became violent and father had to separate us. There was a despair in her way of clinging to me which I could not then understand. I understand it now. I never saw her again.

MARCUS RAVAGE

The Foreigners

Trains bring the foreigners
who get off and look around
    bewildered.
In their eyes swim
frightened fish.
They wear foreign noses,
sad lips.

Nobody picks them up.
They wait for the twilight
that makes no distinctions
then they may visit their relatives
in the Milky Way
in the craters of the moon.

One plays harmonica –
strange melodies.
A different scale inhabits
the instrument,
an unhearable sequence
of lonelinesses.

ROSE AUSLÄNDER

Food for the journey – will there be a buffet?

What provisions are possible on a journey to eternity? The rabbis thought our only luggage would be our good deeds. Everything else would have to be left at the frontier post we call death, which separates this world from eternity.

I gave orders for my horse to be brought round from the stable. The servant did not understand me. I myself went to the stable, saddled my horse and mounted. In the distance I heard a bugle call, I asked him what this meant. He knew nothing and had heard nothing. At the gate he stopped me, asking: "Where are you riding to, master?" "I don't know," I said, "only away from here, away from here. Always away from here, only by doing so can I reach my destination." "And so you know your destination?" he asked. "Yes," I answered, "didn't I say so? Away-From-Here, that is my destination." "You have no provisions with you", he said. "I need none," I said, "the journey is so long that I must die of hunger if I don't get anything on the way. No provisions can save me. For it is, fortunately, a truly immense journey."

FRANZ KAFKA

When you leave Egypt, any Egypt, do not stop to think: "But how will I earn a living out there?" One who stops to make provision for the way will never get out of Egypt.

NACHMAN of Bratslav

O my soul, prepare provisions in abundance, prepare not little while you are yet alive and your hand has strength, because the journey is too great for you. And do not say: "Tomorrow will I make provision", for the day has declined and you know not what the next day may bring.

BACHYA IBN PAKUDA

2 · BUSINESS OF LIFE

Signing our name on cheques and on our lives

In the Bible, a person's name was his being, not just his label, so when his life and being changed, his name changed too. After wrestling with the angel, Jacob (which means "heel", possibly in the modern sense too) became Israel (someone who struggles with God). What's in a name? In tradition quite a lot!

Jacob was left behind alone and a man wrestled with him till the dawn arose. When he saw he could not overcome him he touched the hollow of his thigh and Jacob's thigh was dislocated as he wrestled with him. Then he said: "Let me go, for dawn is breaking." But he said: "I will not let you go unless you bless me." Then he said: "What is your name?" He answered: "Jacob." He said: "No longer shall your name be 'Jacob' (the supplanter) but Israel (striver with God) for you have striven with God and with man and have prevailed."

Genesis 32:25–29

Each man has a name
given him by God
and given him by his father and mother.
   Each man has a name
   given him by his height and his way of smiling
   and given him by his garment.
Each man has a name
given him by the hills
and given him by his walls.
   Each man has a name
   given him by the stars
   and given him by his neighbours.

Each man has a name
given him by his sins
and given him by his longing.
   Each man has a name
   given him by those who hate him
   and given him by his love.
Each man has a name
given him by his festivals
and given him by his work.
   Each man has a name
   given him by the seasons of the year
   and given him by his blindness.
Each man has a name
given him by the sea
and given him
by his death.

ZELDA

Truly You are the one who judges and tests, who probes and bears witness. You record and seal, You count and measure. You remember all that is forgotten. You open the Book of Memory, and it speaks for itself, for everyone has signed it by their life.

HIGH HOLYDAY PRAYER

Making a living

An old Jewish man was hit by a bus. A nice nurse put a pillow under his head and asked, "Are you comfortable, Mr Cohen?" "I make a living, nurse", he whispered reassuringly. "I make a living."

A favourite saying of the Rabbis of Yavneh was: I am God's creature and my fellow is God's creature. My work is in the town and his work is in the country. I rise early for my work and he rises early for his work. Just as he does not presume to do my work, so I do not presume to do his work.

Will you say, I do much and he does little? We have learnt: One may do much or one may do little; it is all one provided he directs his heart to heaven.

Berachot

You don't understand: Willy was a salesman. And for a salesman, there is no rock bottom to the life. He don't put a bolt to a nut, he don't tell you the law or give you medicine. He's a man way out there in the blue, riding on a smile and a shoeshine. And when they start not smiling back – that's an earthquake. And then you get yourself a couple of spots on your hat, and you're finished. Nobody dast blame this man. A salesman is got to dream, boy. It comes with the territory.

ARTHUR MILLER

> He's a one trick pony
> He either fails or he succeeds
> He gives his testimony
> Then he relaxes in the weeds
> He's got one trick to last a lifetime
> But that's all a pony needs
> (that's all he needs)
>
> He looks so easy
> He looks so clean
> He moves like God's
> Immaculate machine
> And it makes me think about
> All of these extra moves I make
> And all this herky jerky motion
> And the bag of tricks it takes
> To get me through my working day

PAUL SIMON

Business people

Ordinary people on their way to work and business.

They tell a story of the Dubner Maggid, the famous preacher of the east European ghettos. Once he was asked by the mighty scholar called the Vilna Gaon to tell him his faults. The Maggid at first declined. When the Gaon pressed him, he at last spoke somewhat like this: "Very well. You are the most pious man of our age. You study night and day, retired from the world, surrounded by the rows of your books, the Holy Ark, the faces of devout scholars. You have reached high holiness. How have you achieved it? Go down in the market place, Gaon, with the rest of the Jews. Endure their work, their strains, their distractions. Mingle in the world, hear the scepticism and irreligion they hear, take the blows they take. Submit to the ordinary trials of the ordinary Jew. Let us see then if you will remain the Vilna Gaon!" They say the Gaon broke down and wept.

HERMAN WOUK

Some people think of business when they are at the Synagogue. Is it too much to ask them to think of God when they are at business?

NACHMAN of Kosov

Market traders

How a trader is true to God! Traditional religious literature preferred to ennoble saints, crusaders, virgins, hermits and ascetics. But they are a bit offbeat for ordinary people like us. Honest traders and businessmen have their own holiness.

It is necessary to be most careful not to deceive one's neighbour. He who deceives his neighbour, whether it is the seller who deceives the buyer, or the buyer who deceives the seller, transgresses a prohibition, for it is written: "And when you sell anything to your neighbour, or when you buy anything from your neighbour, you shall not oppress one another" (Leviticus 25:14). And this is the first question that a man is asked when brought to judgement: "Did you transact your business honestly?"

Just as deception is forbidden in cases of buying and selling so it is prohibited with regard to hiring, contracts, or money changing. If one has something to sell, he is forbidden to make it look better than what it really is in order to deceive thereby. . . .

It is likewise forbidden to mix a little bad food with plenty of good food to sell the same as though they were good, or to mix inferior liquor with superior liquor. But if the taste of the mixed wine be recognized, the mixing is permitted, for the purchaser will detect it.

A shopkeeper is permitted to give parched grain and nuts to children to accustom them to buy from him. He may also sell cheaper than the market price so that people buy from him and the other tradesmen cannot prevent this.

He who gives short measure or weight . . . transgresses a prohibition of the Torah itself, for it is said: "You shall do no unrighteousness in your measures – of length, weight or capacity" (Leviticus 19:35). The punishment of short measures and weights is very severe, for the transgressor cannot repent properly as he does not know how and to whom to make restoration. Even if he institute public charities it is not considered a perfect repentance.

It is necessary to measure and to weigh with a generous eye. . . .

It is necessary to measure according to the customs of the country and no deviation therefrom is permitted. . . . For the Torah has laid down strict rules prohibiting incorrect measures lest a stumbling-block for others arise therefrom.

Kitzur Shulchan Aruch

Wages

"Faithful is your Employer to pay you the reward of your labour"

Sayings of the Fathers 6:5

Ten Cents a Dance (1930)

Verse
I work at the Palace Ballroom,
But gee, that Palace is cheap;
When I get back to my chilly hall room
I'm much too tired to sleep.
I'm one of those lady teachers,
A beautiful hostess, you know,
The kind the Palace features,
For only a dime a throw.

1st Refrain
Ten cents a dance –
That's what they pay me;
Gosh, how they weigh me down!

Ten cents a dance –
Pansies and rough guys,
Tough guys who tear my gown!
Seven to midnight, I hear drums.
Loudly the saxophone blows.
Trumpets are tearing my eardrums.
Customers crush my toes.
Sometimes I think
I've found my hero,
But it's a queer romance.
All that you need is a ticket.
Come on, big boy, ten cents a dance!

Patter
Fighters and sailors and bowlegged tailors
Can pay for their tickets and rent me!
Butchers and barbers and rats from the harbours
Are sweethearts my good luck has sent me.
Though I've a chorus of elderly beaux,
Stockings are porous with holes at the toes.
I'm here till closing time
Dance and be merry, it's only a dime.

Tag
Sometimes I think
I've found my hero,
But it's a queer romance.
All that you need is a ticket.
Come on, big boy, ten cents a dance!

LORENZ HART

You sell yourself as well as your goods in the modern market place. The bitch Goddess of success makes suckers of us all. Even saints aren't safe. Some sell their bodies, some their souls. But sometimes you find someone who won't even take ten cents.

The prayer of a shepherd who "did not know how to pray":
Lord of the Universe! It is apparent and known unto You, that if You had cattle and gave them to me to tend, though I take wages

for tending from all others, from You I would take nothing, because I love You.

Sefer Chasidim

Paying the bill

In Hebrew the same word is used for the bill you pay in a restaurant, and the reckoning you give to God at your last judgement. It is unwise to think the laws of causation will be suspended for you in this world or the next.

What I really wanted to do was to find out how bargaining worked, but whenever I entered the souks I temporarily lost sight of the bargaining for the things that were its object. To the naïve observer there seems to be no reason why a person should turn to one Morocco merchant in particular when there are twenty others beside him whose wares hardly differ from his own. You can go from one to another and back again to the first. Which stall you will buy from is never certain in advance. Even if, say, you have made up your mind to this or that, you have every opportunity of changing it. . . .

In the souks, however, the price that is named first is an unfathomable riddle. No one knows in advance what it will be, not even the merchant, because in any case there are many prices. Each one relates to a different situation, a different customer, a different time of day, a different day of the week. There are prices for single objects and prices for two or more together. There are prices for foreigners visiting the city for a day and prices for foreigners who have been here for three weeks. There are prices for the poor and prices for the rich, those for the poor of course being the highest. One is tempted to think that there are more kinds of prices than there are kinds of people in the world.

ELIAS CANETTI

Rabbi Tarfon says, The day is short, and the work is great, and the labourers are sluggish, and the wages are high, and the Master of the house is insistent.

Sayings of the Fathers 2:20

In debt

The author of this part of the Jewish Grace after Meals seemed to have had a bad experience in life, and it's got frozen into the liturgy. It's true even if it pops up in a peculiar place.

Our God, our father, be our shepherd and feed us, provide for us, sustain us and support us, and relieve us speedily from all our troubles. Let us never be in need of the charity of our fellow men nor their loans, but dependent on Your hand alone which is full, open, holy and ample, so shall we never lose our self-respect nor be put to shame.

GRACE AFTER MEALS

It is forbidden to cross a road to meet a man who is your debtor, and who you know cannot pay you; for it is as if he were tortured with fire and water.

Berachot 6b

Taxes

Don't pay your tithes by a conjectural estimate.
Sayings of the Fathers 1:16

To the highly respected Rabbi Ephraim, member of the great assembly, son of Rabbi Shemarya, of blessed memory, and the Elders, the noble and highly honoured men, may the Lord protect them, from your friends the community of Alexandria, best greetings! . . . You are the supporter of the poor and the aid of people in need, you study diligently, you rouse the good against the evil impulse. You walk in the right way and practise justice. We let you know that we always pray for you. May God grant you peace and serenity!

We turn to you today on behalf of a captive woman who has been brought from Byzantium. We ransomed her for twenty-four denares besides the governmental tax. You sent us twelve denares; we have paid the remainder and the tax. Soon afterwards sailors brought two other prisoners, one of them a fine young man possessing knowledge of the Torah, the other a boy of about ten. When we saw them in the hands of the pirates, and how they beat and frightened them before our own eyes, we had pity on them and guaranteed their ransom. We had hardly settled this, when another ship arrived carrying prisoners. Among them were a physician and his wife. Thus we are again in difficulties and distress. And our strength is overstrained, as the taxes are heavy and the times critical.

Alexandria, first half of the Eleventh Century

They always are, for charity is endless.

Committees

Ministers spend as much time on committees as they spare for people.

Committees are necessary, for when two or three are gathered together not only is God present, so are a potential chairman, secretary and treasurer. But their concern is as much with proceedings and power as with people, so there is always a fight for integrity.

May 19, 1952

Honorable John S. Wood
Chairman
House Committee on Un-American Activities
Room 226 Old House Office Building
Washington 25, D.C.

Dear Mr. Wood:

As you know, I am under subpoena to appear before your Committee on 21 May 1952.

I am most willing to answer all questions about myself. I have nothing to hide from your Committee and there is nothing in my life of which I am ashamed. . .

But I am advised by counsel that if I answer the Committee's questions about myself, I must also answer questions about other people and that if I refuse to do so, I can be cited for contempt. My counsel tells me that if I answer questions about myself, I will have waived my rights under the Fifth Amendment and could be forced legally to answer questions about others. This is very difficult for a layman to understand. But there is one principle that I do understand: I am not willing, now or in the future, to bring bad trouble to people who, in my past association with them, were completely innocent of any talk or any action that was disloyal or subversive. I do not like subversion or disloyalty in any form and if I had ever seen any I would have considered it my duty to have reported it to the proper authorities. But to hurt innocent people whom I knew many years ago in order to save myself is, to me, inhuman and indecent and dishonorable. I cannot and will not cut my conscience to fit this year's fashions. . .

LILLIAN HELLMAN

Committees are places where people keep minutes and waste hours.

MILTON BERLE

Politics

The pragmatic experiences of Jews help deflate the rhetoric of politics and the creation of idols – divine or devilish according to which side you are on.

It is easier to fight for one's principles than to live up to them.

ALFRED ADLER

Why do you sing about the rose? It is the aristocrat of flowers. Why don't you sing the praise of the democratic potato, which is food for the people?

HEINRICH HEINE

If they give you – take; if they take from you – yell!

YIDDISH PROVERB

The essence of peace is to join together two opposites. And do not be alarmed if you see one man who is in complete contrast to your mind (or way of thinking) and you may imagine that it is absolutely impossible to be at peace with him; and also when you see two people who are indeed two opposites (the one to the other); do not say that it may not be possible to make peace between them. On the contrary! That is the essence of the wholeness of peace; to attempt at having peace between two opposites, just as the Lord, blessed be He, makes peace above between fire and water, which are two opposites.

NACHMAN of Bratslav

Rows

Rabbi Menachem Mendel of Lubavitch used to restrain an angry outburst until he had looked into the codes to learn whether anger is permissible in the particular instance. But how much genuine anger could he feel after searching for the authority in the *Shulchan Aruch*!

Chasidic

The Schools of Hillel and Shammai disputed two and a half years whether it would have been better if man had or had not been created. Finally, they agreed that it would have been better had he not been created, but since he had been created, let him investigate his past doings, and let him examine what he is about to do.

Erubin 13b

Said Rab Abba in the name of Samuel: "For three years the Schools of Hillel and Shammai have maintained a controversy, each School asserting that the decision should be given in accordance with its opinion. At last a Voice descended in Jabneh and cried out: 'The words of both these and these are the words of the Living God, but the decision should follow the School of Hillel.'"

Erubin 13b

An insincere peace is better than a sincere war.

YIDDISH PROVERB

A marriage dispute came before a rabbi, he heard the wife patiently. "You are right", he said. The husband intervened, and the rabbi listened to him, and considered carefully. "You are right, too", he said. A bystander shouted out, "If she's right, how can he be right?" The rabbi pondered. "And you're right too", he exclaimed.

Told by LIONEL BLUE

The complexity of modern civilization is a daily lesson in the necessity of not pressing any claim too far, of understanding opposing points of view, of seeking to reconcile them, of conducting matters so that there is some kind of harmony in a plural society.

WALTER LIPPMAN

3 · GOING HOME

In the supermarket

Rabbi Akiba used to say, Everything is given on pledge, and a net is spread for all living. The shop is open, and the shopkeeper gives credit, and the account is open and the hand writes, and whoever wishes to borrow may come and borrow. But the collectors go round every day, and exact payment from man with his consent or without it, and their claims are justified, and the judgement is a judgement of truth. Yet everything is prepared for the feast!

Sayings of the Fathers 3:20

The last line of this section is the most hopeful of religious statements we know; so perhaps the queues, the confusion and hard lessons of this world are worth it.

Yahrzeit Poem

In her later years she took to speaking
Russian once again – strange syllables that we
Had never heard – words long forgotten which found
Their way into her speech by some cerebral
Short-circuit unexplained by science and yet,
After all, only a common miracle.
"It happens all the time", the doctor told us,
And we accepted it and tried to make do only
Half understanding her, hearing sentences
With all the crucial words in an alien tongue.

She never seemed quite at home in the world,
Technology amazed her, and she would spend her
Days staring out the window of her apartment,

Trying, it seemed, to comprehend it all. "What
Does she do all day?" I asked my mother. "She
Counts the cars", my mother replied, as if this
Were a proper activity for an elderly woman,
A simple strategy to order things not understood.

A pious woman, she was unknowingly an animist,
A technological mystic who believed in the souls
Of things. As when our car was stopped at a traffic
Light one day and we fumed, late for some appointment,
She suggested that it was good,
For after all cars too needed to take a rest.

She passed away on a hot July day, and I,
Away on vacation, almost missed hearing
About it: a mixup with the telephones –
It seemed appropriate. She always called
The operator when she wanted a number, a human
Voice helped explain the mystery of bodiless speech.

Today I saw an old woman try to enter a supermarket
The wrong way. She hadn't mastered the electric doors.
What a world for her, I thought, where doors
Never get touched by hands and only open one way.

BARRY HOLTZ

Doctors

When you are sick you only see your own distress not your doctor's. Some of them can't cope or seem gruff, but it is usually defensive. Ministers of religion have the same problem and feel the same anger – but as it must be directed against God they can't express it.

Your eternal providence has appointed me to watch over the life and health of Your creatures. May the love for my art actuate me at all times; may neither avarice nor miserliness, nor the thirst for glory or for a great reputation engage my mind, for the enemies of truth and philanthropy could easily deceive me and make me forgetful of my lofty aim of doing good to Your children. May I never see in a patient anything but a fellow creature in pain. Grant me strength, time and opportunity always to correct what I have acquired, always to extend its domain, for knowledge is immense and the spirit of man can extend indefinitely to enrich itself daily with new requirements.

Today he can discover his errors of yesterday and tomorrow he may obtain new light on what he thinks himself sure of today.

O God, You have appointed me to watch over the life and death of Your creatures. Here I am, ready for my vocation.

MAIMONIDES, *The Medical Oath*

Let us be silent – as silent as the empty houses in the empty streets of our Ghetto. In this prevailing silence lies the power and the depth of our pain and the moans that one day will shake the world's conscience. . . .

A group of medical colleagues, themselves living constantly with the hunger problem, decided that the reality of their every-day grim life should become the subject of our scientific work. Disregarding the terrible conditions, which were completely unsuitable to the work in progress, all of these doctors laboured with utmost devotion and fervour. The hospitals were located in temporary buildings not suitable for the purpose, and lack of apparatus, reagents, and other equipment made the research even more difficult. Many of our physician colleagues themselves suffered from hunger. In spite of this, nobody interrupted the work and quietly, modestly, without any advertising, the work was done. The material collected during five months would have required at least a year under normal conditions. It was as if we knew subconsciously that the work could be interrupted at any minute. . . .

This is the work being published now. It is an "unfinished symphony" full of meaning, written by Jewish doctors in 1942. One detail should not be omitted: the work on the manuscript is being carried out in one of the undestroyed rooms of the cemetery buildings. This is the symbol of our living and working environment. . . .

A few last words to honour you, the Jewish doctors. What can I tell you, my beloved colleagues and companions in misery. You are a part of all of us. Slavery, hunger, deportation, those death figures in our Ghetto were also your legacy. And you by your work, could give the henchman the answer *Non omnis moriar* – "I shall not wholly die".

DR ISRAEL MILEJKOWSKI, Head, Department of
Public Health, Jewish Council in Warsaw,
Warsaw, October 1942

Waiting rooms

Waiting in rooms, corridors, chemists' and surgeries – a foretaste of purgatory in this world.

I pray to You O Lord
From all my heart,
O Lord! I pray to You
With fervour and zeal,
For the sufferings of the humiliated,
For the uncertainty of those who wait;
For the non-return of the dead;
For the helplessness of the dying;
For the sadness of the misunderstood,
For those who request in vain;
For all those abused, scorned and disdained;
For the silly, the wicked, the miserable;
For those who hurry in pain
To the nearest physician;
Those who return from work
With trembling and anguished hearts to their homes;
For those who are roughly treated and pushed aside,
For those who are hissed on the stage;
For all who are clumsy, ugly, tiresome and dull,
For the weak, the beaten, the oppressed,
For those who cannot find rest
During long sleepless nights;
For those who are afraid of Death,
For those who wait in pharmacies;
For those who have missed the train;
– For all the inhabitants of our earth
And all their pains and troubles,
Their worries, sufferings, disappointments,

All their griefs, afflictions, sorrows,
Longings, failures, defeats;
For everything which is not joy,
Comfort, happiness, bliss. . . .
Let these shine for ever upon them
With tender love and brightness,
I pray to You O Lord most fervently –
I pray to You O Lord from the depths of my heart.

JULJAN TUWIM

Rabbi Jacob says, The world is like a corridor to the world to come. Prepare yourself in the corridor so that you may enter the inner chamber.

Sayings of the Fathers 4:21

Waiting room wisdom

In most waiting rooms, people try to comfort each other and allay each other's fears, so there are hints of heaven there. People help each other with humour. They joke and comfort each other with cakes and kind words.

Always Two Possibilities

War was on the horizon. Two students in the *Yeshivah* were discussing the situation.

"I hope I'm not called", said one. "I'm not the type for war. I have the courage of the spirit, but nevertheless I shrink from it."

"But what is there to be frightened about?" asked the other. "Let's analyse it. After all, there are two possibilities: either war will break out, or it won't. If it doesn't, there's no cause for alarm. If it does, there are two possibilities: either they take you or they don't take you. If they don't, alarm is needless. And even if they do, there are two possibilities: either you're given combat duty, or non-combatant duty. If non-combatant, what is there to be worried about? And if combat duty, there are two possibilities: you'll be wounded, or you won't be wounded. Now, if you're not wounded, you can forget your fears. But even if you are wounded, there are two possibilities: either you're wounded gravely, or you're wounded slightly. If you're wounded slightly, your fear is nonsensical, and if you're wounded gravely, there are still two possibilities: either you succumb, and die, or you don't succumb, and you live. If you don't die, things are fine, and there's no cause for alarm; and even if you do die, there are two possibilities: either you will be buried in a Jewish cemetery, or you won't be. Now, if you are buried in a Jewish cemetery, what is there to worry about, and even if you are not . . . but why be afraid? There may not be any war at all!"

Treasury of Jewish Folklore

Tired and fed up on a suburban train

It Was Obvious

A Talmudic scholar from Marmaresch was on his way home from a visit to Budapest. Opposite him in the railway carriage sat another Jew, dressed in modern fashion and smoking a cigar. When the conductor came around to collect the tickets the scholar noticed that his neighbour opposite was also on his way to Marmaresch.

This seemed very odd to him.

"Who can it be, and why is he going to Marmaresch?" he wondered.

As it would not be polite to ask outright he tried to figure it out for himself.

"Now, let me see", he mused. "He is a modern Jew, well dressed, and he smokes a cigar. Whom could a man of this type be visiting in Marmaresch? Possibly he's on his way to our town doctor's wedding. But no, that can't be! That's two weeks off. Certainly this kind of man wouldn't twiddle his thumbs in our town for two weeks!

"Why then is he on his way to Marmaresch? Perhaps he's courting a woman there? But who could it be? Now let me see. Moses Goldman's daughter Esther? Yes, definitely, it's she and nobody else . . . But now that I think of it – that couldn't be! She's too old – he wouldn't have her, under any circumstances! Maybe it's Haikeh Wasservogel? Phooey! She's so ugly! Who then? Could it be Leah, the money-lender's daughter? N – no! What a match for such a nice man! Who then? There aren't any more marriageable girls in Marmaresch. That's settled then, he's not going courting.

"What then brings him?

"Wait, I've got it! It's about Mottel Kohn's bankruptcy case! But what connection can he have with that? Could it be that he is one of his creditors? Hardly! Just look at him sitting there so calmly, reading his newspaper and smiling to himself. Anybody can see nothing worries him! No, he's not a creditor. But I'll bet he has something to do with the bankruptcy! Now what could it be?

"Wait a minute, I think I've got it. Mottel Kohn must have corresponded with a lawyer from Budapest about his bankruptcy. But that swindler Mottel certainly wouldn't confide his business secrets to a stranger! So it stands to reason that the lawyer must be a member of the family.

"Now who could it be? Could it be his sister Shprinzah's son? No, that's impossible. She got married twenty-six years ago – I remember it very well because the wedding took place in the green synagogue. And this man here looks at least thirty-five.

"A funny thing! Who could it be, after all . . . ? Wait a minute! It's as clear as day! This is his nephew, his brother Hayyim's son, because Hayyim Kohn got married thirty-seven years and two months ago in the stone synagogue near the market place. Yes, that's who he is!

"In a nutshell – he is Lawyer Kohn from Budapest. But a lawyer from Budapest surely must have the title 'Doctor'! So, he is Doctor Kohn from Budapest, no? But wait a minute! A lawyer from Budapest who calls himself 'Doctor' won't call himself 'Kohn'! Anybody knows that. It's certain that he has changed his name into Hungarian. Now, what kind of a name could he have made out of Kohn? Kovacs! Yes, that's it – Kovacs! In short, this is Doctor Kovacs from Budapest!"

Eager to start a conversation the scholar turned to his travelling companion and asked, "Doctor Kovacs, do you mind if I open the window?"

"Not at all", answered the other. "But tell me, how do you know that I am Doctor Kovacs?"

"It was obvious", replied the scholar.

Treasury of Jewish Folklore

Delays, breakdowns and industrial disputes

Though these are from the Talmud they are like shaggy dog stories, and are suitable to while away the time in suburban trains which start and stop and hesitate and start again. Whether they are serious or silly is up to you. There is more sly humour in religious writing than reverential readers notice.

The Mouse and the Piece of Bread

On the eve of Passover, the house should be searched to make sure that no leavened bread remains on the premises.

Rava asked a question: "Suppose a mouse entered a room, which had already been searched, with a piece of bread in its mouth, and a mouse then came out of the room with a piece of bread in its mouth. Can one assume that the mouse (and bread) that came out are the same mouse and bread that went in? [In which case no further search is necessary.] Or is it perhaps a different mouse?"

Rava then went on to ask: "Suppose that the answer to my first question is that there is no need to assume a different mouse; what if a white mouse went in with bread in its mouth and a black mouse came out with bread in its mouth? Must one assume that it is a different piece of bread or can one suppose that it is the same piece of bread which the first mouse threw away and the second mouse picked up?

"Perhaps you will say, 'Mice do not take food from each other'. In that case, what if a mouse went in with a piece of bread in its mouth and a weasel came out with a piece of bread in its mouth? Can one assume that the weasel took away the bread from the mouse, or could it be another piece of bread, since a weasel would have the mouse itself in its mouth? Suppose then that the weasel had the mouse *and* the bread in its mouth? But surely (if it were the same piece of bread) the weasel would have the mouse in its mouth and the bread would still be in the mouse's mouth? But perhaps the mouse dropped the bread in its fear and the weasel picked up the mouse and the bread separately?"

The problem was left unsolved.

Pesachim, 10b

Scholars with a feeling for sacred fun are scarce in our time. People are too insecure to cope with such a combination. Hyam Maccoby is an outstanding exception and his book The Day God Laughed, *from which these versions of Talmudic stories are taken, brightens seminaries and his fellow scholars.*

The Rainmaker

Abba Hilkiah was the grandson of Honi the Circle-maker: and when the world needed rain, the Rabbis used to send a delegation to him, and he would pray for rain, and it would come.

Once the world needed rain. The Rabbis sent a pair of rabbis to him to pray for mercy that rain might come. They went to his house and did not find him there. They went into the fields, and found him hoeing. They greeted him with "Peace", but he did not turn his face to them. In the evening, when he had collected some twigs, he set out for home, carrying the twigs and the hoe on one shoulder, and his cloak on the other shoulder.

All the journey he walked barefoot, but when he came to water, he put on his shoes.

When he came to prickly shrubs and brambles, he lifted up his clothes.

When he reached his house, his wife came out to meet him, adorned with ornaments.

His wife went in first, then he went in, and the rabbis went in last.

He sat down to eat, and did not say to the rabbis, "Come, eat with us".

He divided the bread for his children, giving one portion to the elder and two portions to the younger.

Then he said to his wife, "I know that the rabbis have come about rain. Let us go up to the roof and pray for mercy. Perhaps the Holy One, blessed be He, will be pleased to send rain, without any credit being given to us."

They went up to the roof. He stood at one corner of the roof and prayed, and she stood at the opposite corner and prayed. When the rain-clouds appeared, they came first from the direction of her corner.

When he descended from the roof, he turned to the rabbis and said, "Why have the rabbis come?"

They said, "The Rabbis sent us to the Master, that he might ask mercy for rain".

He said to them, "Blessed be the All-present, who has made it unnecessary for you to call on the services of Abba Hilkiah".

They said to him, "We know that the rain came because of the Master. But let the Master tell us these things, at which we wonder: why, when we greeted the Master with 'Peace', did he not turn his face to us?"

He said to them, "I was hired for the day, and I thought I should not spend any of the time in idleness".

"And why did the Master carry the twigs on one shoulder and the cloak on the other?"

He said to them, "It was a borrowed garment. It was lent to act as a cloak, not to carry twigs on it".

"Why did the Master walk all the journey without shoes, but put them on when he came to water?"

He said to them, "All the journey I could see what lay before me, but in the water I could not see what lay before me".

"Why, when the Master came to prickly shrubs or brambles, did he lift up his clothes?"

"Because flesh heals but clothes do not heal."

"Why, when the Master reached his house, did the wife of the Master come out adorned with ornaments?"

He said to them, "So that I would not put my eyes on another woman".

"Why did she go in first, then the Master after her, and we last of all?"

He said to them, "Because you are not well known to me".

"Why, when the Master began to eat, did he not invite us to eat?"

"Because there was not much food, and you would have refrained politely from eating, and I did not want the credit of doing you a favour which was in fact no favour."

"Why did the Master give his elder child one portion of bread, and his younger child two?"

"The elder son stays in the house, and the younger stays all day in the school (where he is not given a meal)."

"And why did the rain-clouds come first from the direction of the corner where the Master's wife was standing?"

"Because she is always in the house and gives bread to the poor who come to the house, and the enjoyment of bread is immediate; while I give money, the enjoyment of which is not immediate. Or perhaps it is because of the bandits who were in our neighbour-hood; I prayed to God that they should die, but she prayed that they should repent."

Ta'anit, 23a

Returning home

We spend much effort on making our homes feel permanent and secure and then see the debris of other people's dreams and homes in charity shops. We have to create our home inside us and in eternity as well. The other homes, like us, cannot last.

I was a child when I entered upon my first journey, in a night which shattered the security of my home. The night had a special name: "Crystal Night" the Nazis called it, the night of smashing the windows of all Jewish shops, of burning the synagogues of Germany, of entering Jewish homes and taking prisoners for the camps. We had been warned by friends, and left our flat, to go into buses, the Underground, and then underground. The next night, my father and I returned to our home, and softly opened the door. We had come home too soon: there was cigar smoke in the hall, and voices in the kitchen. Quietly, we shut the door and walked down the stairs into dark streets. They seemed more comforting and secure than our flat which was no longer our home. I grew up that night. Each step away from a home no longer a home was an assertion of independence, or rather, of a dependence upon my inner self rather than upon outer condi-tions.

In years to come, I would mourn the loss of my innocence. The lesson had come too early and too quickly. "You can only rely on yourself", my father said bitterly. Walking down the quiet streets, with the anger receding behind us and the hiding place near, I thought this was right. I knew too little about myself, and too much about others.

ALBERT FRIEDLANDER

The war is over and people have seen a lot of homes knocked down and now they don't feel safe in their own homes any more, in the way they used to feel safe and snug in them once. Something has happened that they can't get over and years will go by but they will never get over it. So we have lamps lit on our tables again and vases of flowers and portraits of our loved ones, but we don't believe in any of these things any more because once we had to abandon them without warning or scrape around pointlessly for them in the rubble. . . .

When you have been through it once, the experience of evil is never forgotten. Anybody who has seen homes knocked down knows only too well what fragile blessings vases of flowers and paintings and clean white walls are. . . . But we do not go defenceless against this fear. We have a toughness and resilience which others before us never knew. . . . We are forced to go on discovering an inner calm that is not born of carpets and vases of flowers. . . .

There is not one of us who would not love to lay down his head somewhere, to have some snug, cosy little lair to creep into. But there is no peace for the sons of men. There is not one of us who at some time or other has not dreamed of being able to bed down on something soft and comfortable, be soothed, be master of some kind of certainty, some faith or other, and rest. But now the old certainties have all been shattered, and faith has never been just a resting place. . . . But we are bound to this anguish of ours and deep down glad of our destiny as men.

NATALIA GINSBURG (Turin 1946)

For yet another home You have prepared for us, when our time on earth has ended – an eternal home more sure than all the earthly homes that we have known. The stars will soon appear in the dusk. Be our guiding star as we journey into life everlasting. And as the gates of this world close, open again the Gates of Mercy for us, and we shall enter in.

Neilah Service

The Lad Thinks!

The lad thinks – his God is far off in infinity.
The lad becomes a young man – now he seeks God upon
　earth.
Then the grown man – he sees God's Hand in the destiny
　of his fatherland.
And as the father he finds Him in the smile of a child.
And in the quiet little house he discovers how greatly
God's praise has spread in infinity.

And it is well with him who has built his home,
And has recognized God's grace in his quiet walls,
But till one reaches that clear shore so many days pass
Of longing and seeking and youthful torment –
And who can say what is dearer to God,
Knowing Him in the home-tent or seeking Him in the wide
　world?

MENACHEM BOREISHO

A bench in the park

It's a good place to wait for God in the cool of the evening. You are in between the pressures of work and home, and sometimes the person sitting next to you on the bench, whose name you will never know, will say something significant to you.

When I Was Growing Up

When I was growing up, troubled and reckless,
My father told me, God, about You.

But I ran away from You
To play,
For there was so little time.

You
Always wisely kept hidden
So as not to spoil my games,
Till I'd almost forgotten You.

Now as I come back home alone
(All my companions fell asleep along the road)
I've made You out walking beside me,
Old and poor
As I am today.

I'll lend You my stick
As far as a bench in the evening park.
We'll gently inhale the purple sunset
Of far-off skies.
And watch the children playing further
And further away from us.

Then we shall turn to the evening,
We two on our own,
To rest.

DAVID VOGEL

And remember that the companionship of time is of short dura-
tion. It flies more quickly than the shades of evening. We are like a
child that grasps in his hands a sunbeam. He opens his hand soon
again, but, to his amazement, finds it empty and the brightness
gone.

YEDAYA PENINI

Goodlooking people

*They often have problems. Other people are so taken by their "surface"
they don't bother to see their souls.*

Rabbi Johanan said, "I alone remain of the beautiful men of
Jerusalem".

He who desires to see the beauty of Rabbi Johanan should take
a silver goblet while it is still glowing with the heat of the crucible,
fill it with the seeds of red pomegranate, encircle its brim with a
garland of red roses, and set it between the sun and the shade.
That glow gives some impression of the beauty of Rabbi Johanan.

Rabbi Johanan used to go and sit at the gates of the ritual bath.
"When the daughters of Israel ascend from the bath, purified for
intercourse with their husbands," he said, "let them look upon

me, that they may bear sons as beautiful as I, and as learned in the Torah as I."

Baba Metzia 84a

Rabbi Eleazar fell ill, and Rabbi Johanan went to visit him. Rabbi Eleazar was lying in a dark room, but Rabbi Johanan bared his arm, and such was the beauty of Rabbi Johanan that the room became full of light.

Rabbi Johanan then noticed that Rabbi Eleazar was weeping.

"Why do you weep?" he asked. "Is it because you feel that you have not acquired enough knowledge of the Torah in your span of life? Have we not learnt, 'Whether a man achieves much or little, it is all one, as long as he directs his heart to God'?"

Said Rabbi Eleazar, "No; I am weeping because of your beauty, which must one day rot in the earth".

"Ah," said Rabbi Johanan, "for that you are quite right to weep."

So they sat and wept together.

Berachot 5b

The Nazarites were people who vowed to abstain from wine and cutting their hair for a given period. If they broke their vow they had to bring a "guilt offering" to the Temple. Simeon the Just said: I have only once in my life eaten the guilt offering of a Nazarite. Once a man from the south came to me, and I looked at him; he had ruddy cheeks, beautiful eyes and a handsome appearance, and his hair hung from his head in curly locks. I said to him: "Why do you intend to cut off this lovely hair?" He said to me: "I was a shepherd in my city, and I went to fill the trough from the well, and I saw my reflection in the water. Then the evil urge seized me and sought to destroy me from the world. Then I said, you wicked one, why do you boast about that which is not yours, which belongs to the dust, to the worm: I will consecrate you to heaven and I will cut you off for heaven's sake." Then I bowed my head and kissed him, and I said: "Like you, who do the will of God, may there be many in Israel."

Numbers Rabbah Naso 19:7

If the vision of a beautiful woman come suddenly to a man's eyes, or if he perceive any other fair and lovely thing, he should unhesitatingly ask himself: Whence comes this beauty except from the divine force which permeates the world? Consequently the origin of this beauty is divine, and why should I be attracted by the part? Better for me to be drawn after the All, the Source of every partial beauty! If a man taste something good and sweet, let the taster conceive that it is from the heavenly sweetness that the sweet quality is derived. Such perception of beauty then is an experience of the Eternal, blessed be He. . . . Further if he hear some amusing story and he derive pleasure from it, let him bethink himself that this is an emanation from the realm of Love. . . .

BAAL SHEM TOV

Meeting a beggar

Rabbi Moshe Leib said:
"How easy it is for a poor man to depend on God! What else has he to depend on? And how hard it is for a rich man to depend on God! All his possessions call out to him: 'Depend on us!' "

MARTIN BUBER

Brother Can You Spare a Dime

Once I built a railroad, made it run,
Made it race against time.
Once I built a railroad,
Now it's done
Brother can you spare a dime?

Once I built a tower to the sun
Brick and rivet and lime,
Once I built a tower,
Now it's done
Brother can you spare a dime?

Once in khakhi suits,
Gee we looked swell
Full of that Yankee Doodle de-dum.

Half a million boots went sloggin' through
Hell
I was the kid with the drum.
Say, don't you remember
They called me Al,
It was Al all the time,
Say, don't you remember,
I'm your Pal,
Brother can you spare a dime?

E. Y. HARBURG

Living with lodgers

It Could Always Be Worse

The poor Jew had come to the end of his rope. So he went to his rabbi for advice.

"Holy Rabbi!" he cried. "Things are in a bad way with me, and are getting worse all the time! We are poor, so poor, that my wife, my six children, my in-laws and I have to live in a one-room hut. We get in each other's way all the time. Our nerves are frayed and, because we have plenty of troubles, we quarrel. Believe me – my home is a hell and I'd sooner die than continue living this way!"

The rabbi pondered the matter gravely. "My son," he said, "promise to do as I tell you and your condition will improve."

"I promise, Rabbi", answered the troubled man. "I'll do anything you say."

"Tell me – what animals do you own?"

"I have a cow, a goat and some chickens."

"Very well! Go home now and take all these animals into your house to live with you."

The poor man was dumbfounded, but since he had promised the rabbi, he went home and brought all the animals into his house.

The following day the poor man returned to the rabbi and cried, "Rabbi, what misfortune have you brought upon me! I did as you told me and brought the animals into the house. And now what have I got? Things are worse than ever! My life is a perfect hell – the house is turned into a barn! Save me, Rabbi – help me!"

"My son," replied the rabbi serenely, "go home and take the chickens out of your house. God will help you!"

So the poor man went home and took the chickens out of his house. But it was not long before he again came running to the rabbi.

"Holy Rabbi!" he wailed. "Help me, save me! The goat is smashing everything in the house – she's turning my life into a nightmare."

"Go home," said the rabbi gently, "and take the goat out of the house. God will help you!"

The poor man returned to his house and removed the goat. But it wasn't long before he again came running to the rabbi, lamenting loudly,

"What a misfortune you've brought upon my head, Rabbi! The cow has turned my house into a stable! How can you expect a human being to live side by side with an animal?"

"You're right – a hundred times right!" agreed the rabbi. "Go straight home and take the cow out of your house!"

And the poor unfortunate hastened home and took the cow out of his house.

Not a day had passed before he came running again to the rabbi.

"Rabbi!" cried the poor man, his face beaming. "You've made life sweet again for me. With all the animals out, the house is so quiet, so roomy, and so clean! What a pleasure!"

Treasury of Jewish Folklore

Suburban dreams

There is a lot of suffering in the semi's. I found this out for myself when I ministered to middle class suburbs. The bourgeois idea is not big enough to comprehend human happiness. This is not a picture preachers like to present but it's as true.

In My Father's House

Let nobody say I am happy here,
In my father's house I was happier still.
In my father's house I had a lemon-tree
Full grown and in bloom in the month of Adar.

Let nobody say I am happy here.
In my father's house I was happier still.
In my father's house I was well cared for.
In my husband's house I breed and feed.

EDNA SCHWARZ (Translated from
a traditional Spanish poem)

There are days when things, small mechanical things, never cease going wrong. I had such a day today. The washing machine poured water all over the floor. The dishwasher did the same, but it was greasy water to boot. The car wouldn't start. And when, in disgust, I came back into the house to ring the AA and to make a cup of tea, the element in our kettle blew, and I had to boil the water in a saucepan.

All of us have days like that. The sheer frustration makes one want to stamp one's feet, to burst into tears. Things are against us. The slice of bread drops butter down on the floor. And yet in those moments, those intense, angry frustrating moments, there is often a burst of feeling, almost a cliché, that "these are not the things that matter". Forget the machinery. It is people who count. And a person, some person, comes to one's help. AA man, washing machine mechanic, friend, stranger – and the relationship with that person brings us a little nearer a sense of purpose in the world, and beyond.

JULIA NEUBERGER

The eye is not satisfied with seeing

Ecclesiastes 1:8

We expect too much of the world. Our expectations are extravagant in the precise dictionary sense of the word – "going beyond the limits of reason or moderation". They are excessive.

When we pick up our newspaper at breakfast, we expect – we even demand – that it bring us momentous events since the night before. We turn on the car radio as we drive to work and expect "news" to have occurred since the morning newspaper went to press. Returning in the evening, we expect our house not only to shelter us, to keep us warm in winter and cool in summer, but to relax us, to dignify us, to encompass us with soft music and interesting hobbies, to be a playground, a theatre, and a bar. We expect our two-week vacation to be romantic, exotic, cheap, and effortless. We expect a far-away atmosphere if we go to a near-by place and we expect everything to be relaxing, sanitary, and Americanized if we go to a far-away place. We expect new heroes every season, a literary masterpiece every month, a dramatic spectacular every week, a rare sensation every night. We expect everybody to feel free to disagree, yet we expect everybody to be loyal, not to rock the boat or take the Fifth Amendment. We expect everybody to believe deeply in his religion, yet not to think less of others for not believing. We expect our nation to be strong and great and vast and varied and prepared for every challenge; yet we expect our "national purpose" to be clear and simple, something that gives direction to the lives of nearly two hundred million people and yet can be bought in a paperback at the corner drugstore for a dollar.

We expect anything and everything. We expect the contradictory and the impossible. We expect compact cars which are spacious; luxurious cars which are economical. We expect to be rich and charitable, powerful and merciful, active and reflective, kind and competitive. We expect to be inspired by mediocre appeals for "excellence", to be made literate by illiterate appeals for literacy. We expect to eat and stay thin, to be constantly on the move and ever more neighbourly, to go to a "church of our choice" and yet feel its guiding power over us, to revere God and to be God.

Never have people been more the masters of their environment. Yet never has a people felt more deceived and disappointed. For never has a people expected so much more than the world could offer.

DANIEL J. BOORSTIN

Housework

Women's Lib made us see both the here and hereafter from a woman's point of view. It was painful to absorb at times, but the old partial point of view seems so poor and threadbare now.

The protection and preservation of the world against natural processes are among the toils which need the monotonous performance of daily repeated chores. . . . In old tales and mythological stories it has often assumed the grandeur of heroic fights against overwhelming odds, as in the account of Hercules, whose cleansing of the Augean stables is among the twelve heroic "labours". A similar connotation of heroic deeds requiring great strength and courage and performed in a fighting spirit is manifest in the medieval use of the word: labour, *travail*, *Arbeit*. However, the daily fight in which the human body is engaged to keep the world clean and prevent its decay bears little resemblance to heroic deeds, the endurance it needs to repair every day anew the waste of yesterday is not courage, and what makes the effort painful is not danger but its relentless repetition.

HANNAH ARENDT

. . . It is this activity of world-protection, world-preservation, world-repair – the million tiny stitches, the friction of the scrubbing brush, the scouring cloth, the iron across the shirt, the rubbing of cloth against itself to exorcise the stain, the renewal of the scorched pot, the rusted knifeblade, the invisible weaving of a frayed and threadbare family life, the cleaning up of soil and waste left behind by men and children – that we have been charged to do "for love", not merely unpaid, but unacknowledged by the political philosophers. Women are not described as "working" when we create the essential conditions for the work of men; we are supposed to be acting out of love, instinct, or devotion to some higher cause than self.

ADRIENNE RICH

The mother wonders, as she washes the floors furiously, why she does these things, which may be pointless and humiliating: whether she does them in memory of her own mother, or out of some dry, lunatic pleasure. She doesn't do them for love of the house: she realizes that the house means nothing to her. What she cares about are her sons, and their sweet, curly-headed children: people who don't care in the least whether the floors are washed or not.

The mother sits on the sofa, smokes, looks at the olive trees and the vines burning in the midday sun. Everyone comes back, with rubber rings, wet, sand-soaked towels, T-shirts, bits of bread and newspapers: the burden of this slow, happy, indecisive flock. The mother wonders if anyone, once she is dead, will wash the floors.

NATALIA GINSBURG

Tea-time chitchat

People like a little religious chitchat with a priest or pastor over a cosy cup of tea. But you have to be careful the tea doesn't trivialize the subject. A rabbi said: "He loves you, and you love Him, but He is not your pal!" Even if one does not agree, God is not a domestic pet.

It has become fashionable to talk of the relationship between God and man as that of a dialogue. That is as may be; but it should at least be noted that the dialogue involved is not a tea-table conversation. It is rather a call, even a calling to account; and it is curious to observe from the record how some of those called upon found in it terror and suffering and how some, for varying reasons, tried to evade it.

LEON ROTH

In my earlier years the "religious" was for me the exception. . . . "Religious experience" was the experience of an otherness which did not fit into the context of life. . . . The "religious" lifted you out. Over there now lay the accustomed existence with its affairs, but here illumination and ecstasy and rapture held, without time or sequence. . . . The illegitimacy of such a division of the temporal life . . . was brought home to me by an every-day event, an event of judgement. . . . What happened was no more than that one forenoon, after a morning of "religious" enthusiasm, I had a visit from an unknown young man, without being there in spirit. I certainly did not fail to let the meeting be friendly, I did not treat him any more remissly than all his contemporaries who were in the habit of seeking me out about this time of day as an oracle that is ready to listen to reason. I conversed attentively and openly with him – only I omitted to guess the questions which he did not put. Later, not long after, I learned from one of his friends – he himself was no longer alive – the essential content of these questions; I learned that he had come to me not casually, but borne by destiny, not for a chat but for a decision. He had come to me, he had come in this hour. What do we expect when we are in despair and yet go to a man? Surely a presence by means of which we are told that nevertheless there is meaning.

MARTIN BUBER

Gardening

I am grateful to unselfish front gardeners who give so much pleasure to passers by, though they don't sit in them themselves. Front gardens are the loveliest things in suburban London, and often its only beauty.

A Rabbi was once passing through a field where he saw a very old man planting an oaktree. "Why are you planting that tree?" said he. "You surely do not expect to live long enough to see the acorn growing up into an oaktree?"

"Ah," replied the old man, "my ancestors planted trees not for themselves, but for us, in order that we might enjoy their shade and fruit. I am doing likewise for those who will come after me."

Ta'anit

> For thus says the Lord,
> the creator of heaven – He is God;
> who formed the earth and made it – He established it;
> He did not create it as a wasteland,
> but formed it as a place to live.

Isaiah 45:18

When God created the first man, He showed him all the trees in the Garden of Eden. He said to him: "See My works, how fine and excellent they are. All I created I created for you. Think upon this, and do not desolate and corrupt My world; for if you corrupt it, there is no one to set it right after you."

Ecclesiastes Rabbah

Pious potatoes

The menu of a poor Jewish family.

Bulbes

Zuntig – bulbes,
Montig – bulbes,
Dinstig un mitvoch – bulbes,
Donershtig un fraytig – bulbes.
Ober shabes in a novine, a bulbe
    kigele!
Un zuntig vayter, bulbes.

Broyt mit bulbes,
Fleysh mit bulbes,
Varimes un vetshere – bulbes,
Ober un vider – bulbes.
Ober eynmol in a novine a bulbe
    kigele!
Un zuntig vayter bulbes!

Ober – bulbes,
Vider – bulbes,
Ober un vider – bulbes,
Vider un ober – bulbes!
Ober shabes nochn tsholnt a
    bulbe kigele!
Un zuntig vayter, bulbes.

Spuds on Sunday,
Spuds on Monday,
Tuesday and Wednesday –
    spuds!
Thursday and Friday – spuds!
But the treat on the Sabbath is a
    pudding of potatoes!
And on Sunday, once again, it is
    – spuds!

It's bread with spuds
And meat with spuds,
Breakfast and dinner – spuds!
Morning and evening – spuds!
But the special dish is always the
    pudding of potatoes!
And on Sunday, once again, it is
    spuds!

Now – it's spuds
And later – spuds,
Today and tomorrow – spuds!
Week after week, it is spuds!
But the best on the Sabbath is
    the pudding of potatoes!
And on Sunday, once again, we
    get spuds!

But the potato pudding to celebrate the Sabbath can please the rich as well as the poor, just as piety can flourish in poverty. In poor Jewish life it always did. Expense account eating is not a good guide to good cooking or good living.

Potato Kugel

3 eggs
3 cups grated, drained potatoes
⅓ cup potato flour
½ teaspoon baking powder
1½ teaspoons salt
⅛ teaspoon pepper
3 tablespoons grated onion
4 tablespoons melted butter or fat

Beat the eggs until thick. Stir in the potatoes, potato flour, baking powder, salt, pepper, onion and butter or fat.

Turn into a greased 1½-quart baking dish or casserole. Bake in a 350° oven until browned, about 1 hour. Serve hot. Serves 6–8.

JENNIE GROSSINGER

At the Passover meal, Charoseth *represents the mortar with which the children of Israel built the slave cities for Pharaoh. The bitter memory has been transformed into a sweetmeat.*

Charoseth

Apples ½ lb.   *Almonds 2 oz.*
Raisins 2 oz.   *Cinnamon*

Peel and core the apples and chop finely, together with the almonds and raisins. Mix together, adding cinnamon to taste. Then form into a neat block and place in a glass dish, or roll into tiny balls and coat with chopped nuts.

FLORENCE GREENBERG

But even kosher cooking has to keep up with the modern world: thou shalt not consume cholesterol.

Adding Nutrition to Tradition

Chopped liver with grated black radish, moistened with rendered chicken fat and a whisper of chopped onion – pure ecstasy in the mouth. Fluffy knaidlach swimming in chicken soup flecked with gold; hot knishes, crisp and delicious with spicy potato, kasha or cheese fillings; hamantaschen bursting with poppy seeds or prunes; or honey-soaked teiglach or creamy kugels – pure bliss to bite into. Mushroom and barley soup to warm your bones; hearty kasha varnishkas with hot gravy; strudel with heavenly fruit and nut fillings. You don't need a fiddler on the roof to tell you that these foods spell tradition. Their very names evoke blissful memories of small kibitzers crowding around the big black stove, and a lovely warm feeling that Mama's in the kitchen and all's right with the world.

One generation passes, and another takes its place. Now, it's our turn. What kind of memories are we cooking up in our pots and pans? What kind of heavenly aromas say "welcome home" to our loved ones?

Can we, in this age of instant mashed potatoes, TV dinners, frozen blintzes, nondairy creamers, and "foam rubber" bread, provide not only the spirit and spice of Jewish hospitality, but also the nutrients our loved ones need for the lovely glow of health?

Yes, we can!

We can make kugels that are kind to the arteries.

We can put a little heart in all our chopped meat dishes.

We can provide delicious *nosherai* we will be happy to see our families devour because every crumb contributes to health.

We can make fabulous creamy, pareve desserts without resorting to that bag of chemicals called "nondairy creamer".

We can avoid dangerous additives – and save money – by making homemade salad dressings, mayonnaise, yogurt, granolas, and convenience mixes.

We can make delicious honey cakes, mandelbrodt, and strudel without sugar and hydrogenated fats.

We can avoid the hormones and antibiotics in beef by occasionally serving delicious high-protein vegetarian meals.

JANE KINDERLEHRER

"Taste and see that the Lord is good"

Psalm 34:9

Not all Jews came from Eastern Europe and you can get nostalgic about very different sorts of dishes whose taste is lighter than their meaning. Few Christians understand the symbolism of Christmas Pudding, or the origin of a mince pie. I hope this dimension of Jewish cooking doesn't disappear in the same way.

I'm no authority on matters "Indian Jewish", but having been born into a Bene Israel family in Bombay and lived there all my childhood youth, can tell you how we celebrated Rosh Hasha-nah. . . .

Rosh Hashanah was an exciting time, as we always got a new outfit in silk with new shoes etc., and every member of the family was bought a new white handkerchief to be used only for Yom Kippur. Unlike the Jews in the UK, our Rosh Hashanah table was laden with different foods so that by the time dinner was served the children were usually "too full up" to eat.

To start off with there was always sugar instead of salt with the *hamotzi* – then we ate and I don't remember the exact order:

Boiled fish which represented prosperity.

White pumpkin so that we could start off the New Year with a clean sheet.

Boiled beetroot signified the destruction of evil.

Pomegranate so that our year would be as plentiful as the number of seeds in a pomegranate.

Beans so that our good deeds be as many as the beans in each peel (a special long variety of bean).

Honey and apple to have a sweet new year.

Head of lamb or tongue to remind us that Jews should always take the lead, and also a reminder of the sacrifice of Isaac.

Dates to remove from the community all "evil-doers".

Leaves of spring onions (the shape of these resemble a sword) to destroy our enemies.

ELIZABETH ALLAN

Kitchen logic

Rabbi Alexandri said: A man hates to use broken vessels, but God loves them.

Pesikta Shuvah

Love is a fine thing, but love with noodles is even tastier.

YIDDISH PROVERB

Cocktail party thoughts

> Vanity of vanities, all is vanity.
> Ecclesiastes 1:2

The eighth part (at least) of everything
is death. Its weight is not great.
How lightly and with what casual grace
we carry it with us everywhere we go.
On fresh awakenings, on journeys,
or in lovers' talk – though seemingly
left behind in some dark corner –
it is always with us. Weighing
hardly anything at all.

LEAH GOLDBERG

Without God, life is a lonely darkness, even for the man who is in the midst of many other men and even for the man who enjoys pleasures and power. Greater yet than the loneliness of the man who is not understood by his fellow men or who has been cast out by them is the loneliness of the man who knows only his fellow man and only of ties with this earth. It is the loneliness of the man whose soul is far from all that is real, eternal and sublime. In this forlorn state man trembles with despair when he makes answers to those questions about life that he cannot evade.

LEO BAECK

Dinner party

Some people make vows out of hatred of their fellowman, swearing, for example, that they will not let this or that person sit at the same table with them or come under the same roof. Such people should seek the mercy of God, so that they may find some cure for the diseases of their soul.

PHILO

Such people are dreadful to please at dinner parties.

Giving and receiving food are holy actions as can be witnessed in a Jewish Sabbath sanctification and a Christian Eucharist. Giving a meal without at least trying to like your guests is a sort of blasphemy.

If folk knew what others intended for them, they would kill themselves.

YIDDISH PROVERB

One of the hardest things for N.K.V.D. prisoners is to leave over part of the food portion, to cut off a bit of the bread for later. There were many prisoners who could not, under any circumstances, control their hunger, and gobbled up their whole bread ration in the morning without leaving a crumb, and went hungry till next morning. With what envy they regarded their neighbours who were able to divide their bread into three, for the morning, for the midday meal, and for the evening! Time and time again they promised themselves that they would do the same. How many times did they say to themselves: "Only one tiny piece more and I'll keep the rest"? How many times did they break that promise? Just as a drunkard promises himself that each sip will be the last, and takes another sip and yet another, so did these unfortunate people, starved and hungry as they were, nibble away piece after piece until there was nothing left but the waiting for the next bread ration, waiting that devours one's insides.

In every prison cell that I passed through and in every concentration camp hut that I lived in it was possible to divide the prisoners into two categories, as far as the bread was concerned: the wasteful gobblers and the thrifty eaters, but all were hungry. In our small cell, too, we fell into these two categories. The corporal was a waster. He used to promise himself that he would save, but very seldom kept his promise. The officer and I were thrifty. He even broke a record in saving, and I followed his example. We both divided the bread ration not into three, but four (!) portions. We used to leave ourselves a small piece of bread for next day, for the many long hours of the morning between the reveille whistle and the new bread distribution. I am not ashamed to admit that there were many days when my first waking glance was directed upwards to the shelf on which lay a piece of bread the size of an olive. How great was my joy at finding it in its place! And how tasty it was! What do those who eat delicacies know of taste?

MENACHEM BEGIN

Seek no greatness for yourself, no honours, and let your deeds be greater than your learning. Do not long for the table of kings, for your table is greater than theirs, and your crown is greater than theirs.

Sayings of the Fathers 6:5

Dining in heaven or hell

There was a rabbi who wanted to see both Heaven and Hell. And God who has hidden from us the opposites and their unity, gave way to his pleading.

The rabbi found himself before a door, which bore no name, he trembled as he saw it open before him. It gave into a room, and all was prepared for a feast. There was a table, and at its centre a great dish of steaming food. The smell and the aroma inflamed the appetite. The diners sat around the table with great spoons in their hands, yet they were shrieking with hunger, and fainting with thirst in that terrible place. They tried to feed themselves, and gave up, cursing God the author and origin of their torment. For the spoons God had provided were so long that they could not reach their faces and get the food to their tongues. They stretched out their arms, but their mouths remained empty. So they starved because of these spoons while the dish of plenty lay amongst them. And the rabbi knew their shriekings were the cries of Hell. And as knowledge came, the door closed before him.

He shut his eyes in prayer, and begged God to take him away from that terrible place. When he opened them again, he despaired, for the same door stood before him, the door that bore no name. Again it opened, and it gave onto the same room. Nothing had changed, and he was about to cry in horror. There was the table, and at its centre the steaming bowl, and around it were the same people, and in their hands the same spoons.

Yet the shrieking had gone, and the cries and the curses had changed to blessings. And nothing had changed, yet everything. For with the same long spoons they reached to each other's faces, and fed each other's mouths. And they gave thanks to God the author and origin of their joy.

And as the rabbi heard the blessings, the door closed. He bent down, and he too blessed God who had shown him the nature of Heaven and Hell, and the chasm – a hairsbreadth wide – that divides them.

A Taste of Heaven

Card games

A *chasid* complained to Rabbi Zev Wolf of Zbarazh that certain persons were turning night into day, playing cards. "That is good", said the Zaddik. "Like all people, they want to serve God and don't know how. But now they are learning to stay awake and persist in doing something. When they have become perfect in this, all they need do is turn to God – and what excellent servants they will make for Him then!"

A man who had just married off his daughter came running to the rabbi to plead for a divorce.

"What is wrong with the groom?" asked the rabbi.

"He can't play cards."

"What?" cried the rabbi. "Would to God that not a one of our young men could play cards."

"True", said the unhappy father. "But this one does."

Wisdom of Israel

Reading books

Every reader is, while he is reading, the reader of his own self. The writer's work is merely a kind of optical instrument, which he offers to the reader to enable him to discern what, without his book, he would perhaps never have perceived for himself.

MARCEL PROUST

This explains why some very strange books become scriptures. It's not what we can read out of them but what we can read into them. They cannot be read without the human commentary which has grown around them.

Heirloom

My father bequeathed me no wide estates;
No keys and ledgers were my heritage;
Only some holy books with *yahrzeit* dates
Writ mournfully upon a blank front page –

Books of the Baal Shem Tov, and of his wonders;
Pamphlets upon the devil and his crew;
Prayers against road demons, witches, thunders;
And sundry other tomes for a good Jew.

Beautiful: though no pictures on them, save
The Scorpion crawling on a printed track;
The Virgin floating on a scriptural wave,
Square letters twinkling in the Zodiac.

The snuff left on this title page, now brown and old,
The tallow stains of midnight liturgy –
These are my coat of arms, and these unfold
My noble lineage, my proud ancestry!

And my tears, too, have stained this heirloomed ground,
When reading in these treatises some weird
Miracle, I turned a leaf and found
A white hair fallen from my father's beard.

A. M. KLEIN

Do not consider a thing as proof because you find it written in books: for just as a liar will deceive with his tongue, he will not be deterred from doing the same thing with his pen. They are utter fools who accept a thing as convincing proof simply because it is in writing.

MAIMONIDES

Writing books

Everyone has a sermon within them – a secret scripture, the story of their own life as they alone know it. It doesn't have to be published to be important.

See, I come, carrying a book, telling the story of my life.

Psalm 40:8

Some of my friends and acquaintances who know the secret of my diary urge me, in their despair, to stop writing. "Why? For what purpose? Will you live to see it published? Will these words of yours reach the ears of future generations? How? If you are deported you won't be able to take it with you because the Nazis will watch your every move, and even if you succeed in hiding it when you leave Warsaw, you will undoubtedly die on the way, for your strength is ebbing. And if you don't die from lack of strength, you will die by the Nazi sword. For not a single deportee will be able to hold out to the end of the war."

And yet in spite of it all I refuse to listen to them. I feel that continuing this diary to the very end of my physical and spiritual strength is a historical mission which must not be abandoned. My mind is still clear, my need to record unstilled, though it is now five days since any real food has passed my lips. Therefore I will not silence my diary.

HAYYIM KAPLAN

Lullabies

Jewish children are given a lot of love but not much protection against premature knowledge of life's problems. Though I was rocked to sleep by such songs I now find them off-putting though wise. There's too many tears for a tiny tot.

Yankele

Sleep, Yankele, my darling little baby,
Shut your big black eyes.
A big boy who has all his teeth,
Ought Mother sing him lullabies?

A big boy who has all his teeth,
And will go to school by and by,
And study Torah and Talmud,
Ought he, when his mother rocks him, cry?

A big boy who soon will study Talmud,
While father stands by, nodding happily.
A big boy, who's growing up a scholar,
Ought he nights not let his mother be?

A big boy growing up a scholar,
And an enterprising merchant yet.
A big boy who will make a nice girl happy,
Ought he to be lying here so wet?

Sleep then, sleep, my groom that is to be,
Right now you're in the cradle, sad but true –
It will cost much toil and many tears,
Before anything becomes of you!

MORDKHE GEBIRTIG

Going to bed

Angels around my head.
   Fortunately the angels survive, though only just, in modern Judaism, which has been concerned with the material problems of this world not the mystical means to the next. This still makes many people secure before they sleep. It's a good exit after a hard day – or a hard life.

In the name of the Lord God of Israel, may Michael, the protection of God, be at my right hand; and Gabriel, the power of God, at my left; before me Uriel, the light of God; behind me Raphael, the healing of God; and above my head Shechinat El, the presence of God.

My Mother's Prayer at Night

Lord, let Your light be only for the day,
And the darkness for the night.
And let my dress, my poor humble dress
Lie quietly over my chair at night.

Let the church bells be silent,
My neighbour Ivan not ring them at night.
Let the wind not waken the children
Out of their sleep at night.

Let the hen sleep on its roost, the horse in the stable
All through the night.
Remove the stone from the middle of the road
That the thief may not stumble at night.

Let heaven be quiet during the night,
Restrain the lightning, silence the thunder,
They should not frighten mothers giving birth
To their babies at night.

And me too protect against fire and water,
Protect my poor roof at night.
Let my dress, my poor humble dress
Lie quietly over my chair at night.

NACHUM BOMZE

A Life

Plan for this world as if you were to live forever;
plan for the world to come as if
you were to die tomorrow.

IBN GABIROL

4 · LIVING

This is your life

In many synagogues the sense of the liturgy is sung away by combined cantors and choirs. This is human and understandable. On their own the words are stark, simple and chilling.

We declare how profound is the holiness of this day, for it arouses in us the deepest awe. Today the power of Your kingdom stirs within us. Love is the foundation of Your throne, and the spirit of truth rests upon it.

Truly You are the one who judges and tests, who probes and bears witness. You record and seal, You count and measure. You remember all that is forgotten. You open the Book of Memory, and it speaks for itself, for every man has signed it by his life.

The great *shofar* sounds, and a still small voice is heard. God's messengers feel the alarm. Also possessed by fear and trembling, they announce: "Behold the Day of Judgement!" For judgement comes upon the heavens as well as the world, for neither can stand before Your judgement. This day all who enter the world pass before You like a flock of sheep. And as a shepherd gathers his flock and makes them pass beneath his staff, everything that lives passes in front of You, and You record, and count, and consider them. You set a limit to the life of every creature, and determine its destiny.

On Rosh Hashanah we consider how judgement is formed,
on Yom Kippur we consider how judgement is sealed,

for all who pass away and all who are born, for all who live and all who die, for those who complete their normal span and those who do not – who perish by fire or water, by the violence of man or the beast, by hunger or thirst, by disaster, plague or execution; for those who rest and those who wander, for the secure and the tormented, for those who become poor and those who become rich, for the failures and the famous.

Yet repentence and prayer and good deeds can transform the harshness in our destiny.

Unetanneh Tokef Prayer,
Day of Atonement Liturgy

What is this life?

Lord, hear! Lord, pardon! Lord, listen and act! What are we? What is our life? What is our love? What is our justice? What is our success? What is our endurance? What is our power? Lord our God, and God of our ancestors, what can we say before You, for in Your presence are not the powerful as nothing, the famous as if they had never existed, the learned as if without knowledge, and the intelligent as if without insight.

Siddur

I used to think these questions from the morning liturgy were rhetorical – normal pious overstatements. I have come to consider them factually – like the questions on income tax forms. It is worthwhile keeping a record of our answers. As they change, they indicate what is changing within us.

Strange now to think of you, gone without corsets and eyes,
    while I walk on the sunny pavement of Greenwich Village.
downtown Manhattan, clear winter noon, and I've been up
    all night, talking, talking, reading the Kaddish aloud,
    listening to Ray Charles blues shout blind on the
    phonograph the rhythm the rhythm – and your memory in my head
    three years after – And read Adonais' last triumphant stanzas
    aloud – wept, realizing how we suffer –
And how Death is that remedy all singers dream of . . .
    . . . as I walk toward the
    Lower East Side – where you walked fifty years ago, little
    girl – from Russia, eating the first poisonous tomatoes
    of America – frightened on the dock –

then struggling in the crowds of Orchard Street toward what?
  – toward Newark –
toward candy store, first home-made sodas of the century, hand-
  churned ice cream in backroom on musty brown floor-
  boards –
Toward education, marriage, nervous breakdown, operation,
  teaching school, and learning to be mad, in a dream –
  what is this life?

ALLEN GINSBERG (from Kaddish)

Growing up

Religion has to grow up otherwise believers become better than the God they believe in. I think this is the meaning of this strange story tucked away in the Talmud. It may be a spiritual virtue to be childlike. To remain childish, when you have passed it, does no good to anybody, least of all yourself.

On a certain occasion Rabbi Eliezer used all the arguments in the world to prove his opinion on a point of law but the Rabbis did not accept it. Finally he said: "If I am right about this law, let this carob tree prove it." The carob tree uprooted itself and moved from its place a hundred cubits (some say four hundred cubits). The Rabbis said to him: "No proof can be brought from a carob tree!" Rabbi Eliezer said: "If I am right about this law, let this stream prove it." Then the stream turned about and flowed backwards. The Rabbis said to him: "No proof can be brought from a stream." Rabbi Eliezer said: "If I am right about this law, let the walls of this House of Study prove it." The walls of the House of Study began to bend inwards as if about to fall. Rabbi Joshua rebuked them, saying: "If the students of the wise are disputing about the law, what does it have to do with you!" Out of respect for Rabbi Joshua the walls did not fall, but out of respect for Rabbi Eliezer they did not straighten up, and remain bent to this day. Rabbi Eliezer said: "If I am right about this law, may proof come from heaven." A voice came from heaven and said: "What have you to do with Rabbi Eliezer? On every occasion his is the right interpretation of the law." Rabbi Joshua stood up and said: " 'It is not in heaven' (Deuteronomy 30:12)." What did he mean by using this quotation? Rabbi Jeremiah said: "The Torah was already given to us on Mt Sinai. We pay no attention to a heavenly voice for You have already written in the Torah at Mt Sinai: 'Decide according to the majority' (Exodus 23:2 – as interpreted by the Rabbis)." Rabbi Nathan met the prophet Elijah and asked him: "What did the Holy One, blessed be He, do in that hour?" Said Elijah: "He was laughing and saying: 'My children have defeated Me! My children have defeated Me!' "

Baba Metzia 59b

It was in Buchenwald that I learnt from Jews, Christians, Moslems and pagans, from Englishmen, Serbs, Rumanians, Albanians, Poles and Italians that I was only one more suffering insignificant man; that the tongue my mother taught me, and my Hungarian memories and the traditions of my nation, were nothing but artificial barriers between myself and others. For essentially, as Mankind, we are one. A slap in the face hurts an Englishman as much as it does a German, a Hungarian or a Negro. The pain is the same; only our attitude to the pain differs according to the culture pattern of the country and the individual. Our dreams, each dreamt in a different language, spell out the same dream in the language of Mankind: all of us want peace, security, a life free from fear. And each in his own way, irrespective of differences of nationality or race, we seek for the meaning – or meaninglessness – of life and death, believe in God or deny Him, cry for a woman on whose bosom we may rest our tormented head. . . .

I learnt that within me, as in others, the murderer and the humanitarian exist side by side; the weak child with the voracious male. That I am not in any way superior, that I am not different from others, that I am but a link in the great chain, was among the greatest discoveries of my life. From then on I resolved to support those who fell, even as I had been supported. When someone was despicable, greedy and selfish, I remembered all the occasions when I, too, had been despicable, greedy and selfish. Buchenwald taught me to be tolerant of myself, and by that means tolerant of others. It may be that I would have learnt this without the lesson of Buchenwald. But I would have learnt it much later – perhaps too late.

EUGENE HEIMLER

Dilemmas of daily life and problems posed by Scriptures

They are like the horizon – they don't disappear. But though you can't solve them, you become wise and learn to live with them.

And Adam knew Eve his wife and she conceived and bore Cain, saying: "I have gained a male child with the help of the Lord." Again she gave birth, to his brother Abel. Abel became a tender of sheep and Cain a tiller of the soil. In the course of time Cain brought an offering to the Lord from the fruit of the soil, then Abel, in turn, brought the choicest of the firstborn of his flock. The Lord looked with favour upon Abel and his offering, but to Cain and his offering He showed no favour. So Cain was very angry and downcast. Then the Lord said to Cain: "Why are you angry and why so downcast? If you do well it can be borne; but if you do not do well sin is the demon at the door, hungering for you, and you must master it!"

Then Cain began speaking to Abel his brother . . . and when they were out in the field Cain rose up against Abel his brother and killed him. Then the Lord said to Cain: "Where is Abel your brother?" And he said: "I do not know. Am I my brother's keeper?"

Genesis 4:1–9

Power over others.

Do not trust in yourself until the day of your death.

HILLEL (Sayings of the Fathers 2:5)

The Lord sent Nathan to David. When he came to him he said: "There were two men in a certain city, one rich, the other poor. The rich man had flocks and herds in great numbers. But the poor man had nothing but a single little ewe-lamb which he had bought and fed and raised with his own children – it ate his bread, drank from his cup and lay in his arms, as precious to him as a daughter. Once a traveller visited the rich man, who did not care to take from his own flocks and herds to provide for the guest who had visited him, so he took the lamb of the poor man instead and provided it for his guest."

Then David was enraged at the man and said to Nathan: "As the Lord lives, the man who would do such a thing deserves to die! He shall pay four times over for the ewe-lamb for doing this and being so uncaring!"

Then Nathan said to David: "You are the man!"

2 Samuel 12:1–7

Questioned by life

What was really needed was a fundamental change in our attitude toward life. We had to learn ourselves and, furthermore, we had to teach the despairing men in the concentration camp, that it did not really matter what we expected from life, but rather what life expected from us. We needed to stop asking about the meaning of life, and instead to think of ourselves as those who were being questioned by life – daily and hourly.

VIKTOR E. FRANKL

Living with handicaps

All humans are marred by flaws, which may distort their psyches and impair the way they conduct their lives. However, unless the person is disabled, such flaws and blemishes remain a private matter. The flaws and blemishes of the disabled are visible; indeed, this is a working definition of disability. Disabilities are public property. Any member of the public may ponder about, relate to, write scholarly or popular articles about, dream about, fantasize about another person's disability without accepting responsibility towards that person. When this happens, the disabled person becomes a symbol or an image in the eyes of the beholder; he is no longer a person, but is an object. Furthermore, the meaning of the image or the symbol is largely independent of the person-object. It is determined by external variables, such as the prevalent attitudes of society and the psychic needs of the beholder.

JONATHAN OMER-MAN

Blessing to be recited on seeing people of unusual appearance:
Blessed are You, Lord our God, king of the universe, who
varies the forms of creation.

Siddur

Prejudice

For you were strangers in the land of Egypt.

Leviticus 19:34

A man came to a Polish magnate and asked him: "What do you
think of the Jews?" The answer was: "Swine, Christ-killers,
usurers, not to be trusted." "But what do you think of Isaac?" "A
man after my own heart. An honourable man. A kind man. He
saved me from bankruptcy." "And what do you think of Berl?" "I
have known Berl all my life. He's one of the best." "And of
Shmuel?" "Shmuel is a saint as everyone knows."

The same man went to a rich and pious Jew and asked him:
"What do you think of the Jews?" The pious man answered: "A
kingdom of priests and a holy nation, the elect of the Eternal,
blessed be his name." "And what do you think of Isaac?" "That
thief? That scoundrel? May his bones be broken. He looks at you
and you are robbed!" "And of Berl?" "A fellow of the same kind,
without truth or justice." "And of Shmuel?" "Do you think I am
taken in by his piety? A pretentious idiot."

LUDWIG LEWISOHN

One midnight when Rabbi Moshe Leib was absorbed in the
mystic teachings, he heard a knock at his window. A drunken
peasant stood outside and asked to be let in and given a bed for
the night. For a moment the zaddik's heart was full of anger and
he said to himself: "How can a drunk have the insolence to ask to
be let in, and what business has he in this house!" But then he
said silently in his heart: "And what business has he in God's
world? But if God gets along with him, can I reject him?" He
opened the door at once, and prepared a bed.

MARTIN BUBER

This book is for my father, who died long ago. Once, when I was small, about eight, I was with my father, who was a loving man, in a narrow street in the East End. A huge labourer suddenly roared down at us that we had killed Jesus. My father asked him why he was so unhappy, and the fist lowered and the shouting stopped and he began to cry. We took him with us to my aunt for tea. This book is for my father, who was a loving man.

DAVID KOSSOFF

Scapegoats

An old religious ritual from the time of the Temple and some spiritual images from the Middle Ages foreshadow the methods of modern therapy and psychoanalysis. They provide a clue to understand prejudice – our own and others'.

"And he sent the live goat with an appointed man, who led it into the wilderness. Then the High Priest made the offering for himself and his people, to atone for himself and for his people."

As we remember the scapegoat for Azazel, an animal led to the wilderness, we remember the sins for which we have not atoned, the evil whose consequences remain, the people who have not prayed, the terrible things that have been done in ignorance, the scarlet thread of shame in our life, and all that remains unreconciled to You. They are not cast into the depths of the sea, and no goat now takes them to the wilderness, but You can bring them into oblivion, and repair all that remains undone. May this be Your will.

High Holyday Machzor

Do not reproach your fellow for a blemish that is in you.

RASHI

Sinners are mirrors. When we see faults in them, we must realize that they only reflect the evil in us.

BAAL SHEM TOV

We hate the criminal and deal severely with him because we view in his deed, as in a distorting mirror, our own criminal instincts.

SIGMUND FREUD

I felt angry with fate at having to share my compartment with a German. I knew that he was too young to have had any part of the hideous past, that he was a nice well-mannered lad; and yet I could not help feeling hostile and resentful towards him. I hated him because of his race, and I was ashamed of it. How could I of all people hate someone because of his race? (When we spoke I answered him harshly: "*Jawohl!*")

As soon as I had said it I was sorry. By using the German word I had tried to humiliate him. My desire to humiliate this young man was causing me to feel guilty, and yet at the same time I asked myself why I should feel hurt for wanting to hurt the German. Then it occurred to me that this was the argument of the SS; to hurt, to kill the Jew is not a sin; it is an act of delousing. The feelings I was experiencing were not my own feelings, but theirs. I felt confused. I was doing to him what they had done to me. I was persecuting an innocent man whose only sin was that he happened to be born in Germany.

EUGENE HEIMLER

Projection is the human propensity to find a scapegoat and to see in that scapegoat all the unpleasant things we fail to recognize in ourselves. This mechanism is one of the few unchallenged laws on which all schools of psychology agree, i.e. that if unconscious ideas and emotions are not made conscious, they are *projected* onto our environment where the flimsiest of hooks can carry them. It is the process, *par excellence*, on which thrive opposing political parties and enemy nations; and we can see it in operation in every personal imbroglio, especially in family complications. . . .

We need each other to grow and to fulfil our true selves, on condition that we take the long and arduous path of sincerely trying to find out *who we are*.

MOLLY TUBY

Passing the buck

Strange scapegoats!

One of the ways in which some prisoners tried to protect their integration was to feel newly important because their suffering protected others. After all, concentration camp prisoners had been singled out for punishment by the SS as representative of all the dissatisfied elements.

This having to suffer for others was used by many prisoners to pacify inner guilt over their antisocial behaviour in the camps, while the actually unbearable living conditions were used to rationalize such behaviour toward others. Indications of this were to be found whenever one prisoner called another one to task for misbehaviour . . . the typical response was: "I can't be normal when I have to live in such circumstances."

By a parallel reasoning they felt they had atoned for any shortcomings in the past, whether in themselves or in their relations to family and friends, as well as any future changes they might still undergo. They felt free to deny responsibility or guilt on a number of scores, felt free to hate other people, including their own families, even where the shortcomings were obviously their own. . . .

Such defences, aimed at retaining self-respect by denying all guilt, actually weakened the prisoners' personalities: by blaming outside forces for their actions, they not only denied having personal control of their lives, but also that what they did was of any consequence. Blaming others, or outside conditions for one's own misbehaviour may be the child's privilege; if an adult denies responsibility for his actions, it is another step toward personality disintegration.

BRUNO BETTELHEIM

The Lord spoke to Moses: "Go down, for *your* people whom *you* led out of Egypt have gone astray!" . . . Then Moses appealed to the Lord his God and said: "O Lord, why are You angry with *Your* people whom *You* brought out of the land of Egypt?!"

Exodus 32:7,11

(The use of "your" is a giveaway on both sides – human and divine, like parents disowning their children, shifting responsibility from themselves to each other, when their offspring are naughty.)

The soul when accustomed to superfluous things acquires a strong habit of desiring others which are necessary neither for the preservation of the individual nor for that of the species. This desire is without limit; whilst things which are necessary are few, and restricted within certain bounds. Lay this well to heart, reflect on it again and again; that which is superfluous is without end (and therefore the desire for it is also without limit). Thus you desire to have your vessels of silver, but golden vessels are still better; others even have vessels studded with sapphires, emeralds, or rubies. Those, therefore, who are ignorant of this truth, that the desire for superfluous things is without limit, are constantly in trouble and pain. When they thus meet with the consequences of their course they complain of the judgement of God; they go so far as to say that God's power is insufficient, because He has given to this universe the properties which they imagine cause these evils.

MAIMONIDES

Taking responsibility

We who lived in concentration camps can remember the men who walked through the huts comforting others, giving away their last piece of bread. They may have been few in number, but they offer sufficient proof that everything can be taken from a man but one thing: the last of the human freedoms – to choose one's attitude in any given set of circumstances, to choose one's own way.

And there were always choices to make. Every day, every hour, offered the opportunity to make a decision, a decision which determined whether or not you would become the plaything of circumstances, renouncing freedom and dignity to become moulded into the form of the typical inmate.

VIKTOR E. FRANKL

If I am not for myself, who is for me? But if I am only for myself, what am I? And if not now, when?

HILLEL

Promises, promises!

Inflated money isn't worth much in this life, and inflated promises no more in the next! It's better to start with the small stuff which is solid.

Said the "Yud": "Accustom yourself to generosity by degrees. At first refuse not a request for a pinch of snuff, for the light of a match, or for other small gifts. Such petty kindnesses will broaden your heart so that you can acquire the habit of helping your fellowman in greater ways."

Chasidic

Even vows for charity are not desirable. If one has money, let him give it at once without a vow; and if not, let him wait until he has it.

Shulchan Aruch

When you make a promise to God, do not delay in fulfilling it, for He has no pleasure in fools. Whatever you vow fulfil. It is better not to vow than to vow and not fulfil. Let not your mouth cause guilt to your body and plead before the collector "it was just a mistake". Why should God be angry at your speech and destroy what you have achieved?

Ecclesiastes 5:3–5

Do not tell the collector "it was just a mistake". This refers to someone who makes a public pledge to charity and then refuses to pay. Do not tell the charity collector when he comes: "I did not really mean what I said. My pledge was not meant to be taken in earnest. I only spoke out ih order to avoid public embarrassment or so that others may pledge; but I did not and I do not intend to give any of my own money." Or perhaps you will say: "I did not know what I was doing." Or: "At the time I made the pledge I was confident I would be able to pay but now I find I cannot." None of these excuses will be acceptable to God.

Midrash Psalms

5 · LOVE

Confirmation in the back row of the cinema

Children are confirmed in churches and synagogues. But it was in the back rows of cinemas and other unrecognized venues that we began to confront the passions and perplexities of adult life. We had little guidance, for grown-ups were inadequate and evasive.

Only Me
for Ingrid Bergman

And now you'll never know
that our lives
were once
so closely intertwined.
On a drizzly Saturday night
in the back row of the "Cosmo"
– there we were –
You and Gary Cooper,
me and Leon Goldbloom. . . .
And as you manoeuvred
your first awkward kiss
– so did we.
And later, floating into
the reality
of Sauchiehall Street,
sucking peppermint lumps
and holding sticky hands,
we were still
in your enchanted embrace.

Now you and Gary are gone
and Leon never returned
from Korea –
So, it's only me.

ANNA SOTTO-BOLGAR

Set me as a seal upon your heart,
as a seal upon your arm;
for love is strong as death.

Song of Songs 8:6

Being stood up

Sex is obsessive as it makes people self-centred. People in love often think their love or lack of it excuses their broken promises and appointments. Such failures are usually the result of inadequacy not villainy.

When love was strong, we could have made our bed on a sword's blade; now, when it has become weak, a bed of sixty cubits is not large enough for us.

Sanhedrin

The night is bitter,
The stars have lost their glitter;
The winds grow colder
And suddenly you're older –
And all because of the man that got away.

No more his eager call,
The writing's on the wall;
The dreams you've dreamed have all
  Gone astray.

The man that won you
Has run off and undone you.
That great beginning
Has seen the final inning.
Don't know what happened. It's all a crazy game.

No more that all-time thrill,
For you've been through the mill –
And never a new love will
  Be the same.

Good riddance, good bye!
Ev'ry trick of his you're on to.
But, fools will be fools –
And where's he gone to?

The road gets rougher,
It's lonelier and tougher.
With hope you burn up –
Tomorrow he may turn up.
There's just no let-up the live-long night and day.

Ever since this world began
There is nothing sadder than
  A one-man woman looking for
  The man that got away . . .
  The man that got away.

IRA GERSHWIN

If two lie together they can keep each other warm, but how can one keep warm by himself?

Ecclesiastes 4:11

There's something wrong with the supply and demand of spirituality. There's lots of it in synagogues or churches, when you don't much need it, and not enough when you're almost dying of disappointment and waiting lonely at a bus stop.

Waiting

Waiting for someone
who does not appear
is a quite special skill.

Of course it depends
how much is invested
in the meeting
but the salient points
remain the same.

How late is late?
When does doubt
become unease
become certainty?
How many others
have similar vigils
nearby?

How soon
does the casual awareness
of another's tardy partner
elicit hopes or fantasies
to be dashed
when he appears?

Double-dashed.

Those who wait
know
in their heart of hearts
it was a mistake
mischance
easily remedied.

So the smile,
though strained,
remains.
Some gestures
tell indifferent passers-by
that nothing is amiss.

A last casual glance
at the watch,
tap it, perhaps.

Offer the nearest
now familiar face
a reassuring glance
and limp
into the setting sun.

JONATHAN MAGONET

Comment

Oh, life is a glorious cycle of song,
A medley of extemporanea;
And love is a thing that can never go wrong;
And I am Marie of Rumania.

DOROTHY PARKER

Boy loses girl

In the days of the great migrations, only letters linked the emigrants to those they loved whom they would never see again. It happened to Irish and Jews in steerage to America, to Britons trying their luck on the long passage to Australia, and Welshmen to Argentina.

Oy, Dortn, Dortn, Ibern Vasserl

Oh there, there, across the water
Oh there, there, across the bridges
You have sent me away to distant lands
And I yearn to be back with you.

Oh how many evenings did we sit together?
Oh how many evenings, late into the night?
Oh how many tears have we shed
Till we have told each other of our love?

Oh help me God, God in heaven,
Oh help me God in my pain.
For three long years we have loved each other
But our love cannot be fulfilled.

Oh your eyes, like black cherries
And your lips, like pink paper
And your fingers, like ink and a quill
Oh you should write so many letters to me.

TRADITIONAL YIDDISH

True love

If love depends on some selfish cause when the cause disappears love disappears; but if love does not depend on a selfish cause it will never disappear. What love depended on a selfish cause? Amnon's love for Tamar (2 Samuel 13). What love did not depend on a selfish cause? David's love for Jonathan (1 Samuel 18).

Sayings of the Fathers 5:19

You can look them up yourself! There is much to be learnt from these parts of scripture which are not normally read in places of worship.

Everyone has in his life a beautiful day when, like the first human beings in Eden, he finds love without care and trouble. But when this day is past, you earn love, as you earn bread, by the sweat of the brow.

LUDWIG BOERNE

Expressions of love

The most moving statements of love in the Hebrew scriptures are reserved for that comic figure the mother-in-law and the love between two men.

Then Naomi said: "Go back, my daughters, why do you go with me? Do I still have sons in my womb to become your husbands! Go back, my daughters, go, for I am too old to be with a man. If I were to say that I had hope, even if I was this very night with a man, even if I bore sons, would you wait for them till they grew up, would you shut yourselves up for them, never being with a man?! No! my daughters, for my lot is more bitter than yours, for the hand of the Lord has come out against me." And they raised their voice and wept again. Then Orpah kissed her mother-in-law, but Ruth clung to her. So she said: "Look, your sister-in-law has gone back to her people and her God, go back after your sister-in-law."

But Ruth said: "Do not urge me to leave you, to go back from following you; for wherever you go, I will go, and wherever you lodge I will lodge, your people are my people and your God my God. Where you die I will die and there I shall be buried. May the Lord do so to me and more if anything but death separate me from you."

Ruth 1:11–17

> Saul and Jonathan,
> Loved and beautiful in their lives,
> And in their deaths they were undivided –
> They were swifter than eagles,
> Stronger than lions.
>
> O daughters of Israel,
> Weep for Saul,
> Who clothed you in scarlet with fineries,
> Who added a gold ornament to your clothing.
>
> How have the heroes fallen
> In the midst of war!
> Jonathan,
> On your high places slain!
>
> It is hard for me,
> My brother Jonathan;
> You were very beautiful to me.
> Your love was more wondrous to me
> Than the love of women.
>
> David's Lament for Jonathan
> 2 Samuel 1:23–27

The passage in praise of a virtuous wife, which ends the Book of Proverbs, is noble, but seems to lack the ecstasy of the former.

> A woman of worth, who can find her,
>   for she is more precious than rubies.
> Her husband trusts her in his heart
>   and has no loss by it.
> Every day of her life
>   she does him good, not harm.
> Her hand is held out open to the poor,
>   reaching out to those in need.

> She is clothed in dignity,
>   serene before the time to come.
> When she speaks, it is with wisdom
>   and on her tongue is the guidance of love.
> She looks after the home with care,
>   and does not idle away her time.
> Her children stand up and honour her,
>   and her husband sings her praises.
> "Many a woman has done splendid deeds,
>   but you surpass them all."
> Charm deceives and beauty fades,
>   so praise the woman who honours God.
> Give her honour for the work of her hands,
>   and her own good deeds will praise her in public.
>
> Proverbs 31

Love is less "natural" in families than simple sermons on family life suppose. You learn and earn it the hard way. You have to supplement sentiment with understanding – of real people not your projections.

Then something snapped within me; my lone and woeful childhood, my tormented adolescence, my joyless youth – I flung these all into father's face. He stood aghast as I denounced him, emphasizing every charge by beating my scrubbing-brush on the floor. Every cruel incident of my life stood out in my arraignment. Our large barn of a home, father's angry voice resounding through it, his ill-treatment of the servants, his iron grip on my mother – everything that had haunted my days and terrorized my nights I now recalled in my bitterness. . . . My words rushed on like a torrent, the brush pounding the floor with all the hatred and scorn I felt for my father. The terrible scene ended with my hysterical screams. My brothers carried me up and put me to bed. The next morning I left the house. I did not see father again before I went to New York.

I had learned since then that my tragic childhood had been no exception, that there were thousands of children born unwanted, marred and maimed by poverty and still more by ignorant misunderstanding. . . .

My father's end, though not unexpected, affected me deeply.

. . . An invalid for over thirty years, he had of late been more frequently ill than usually. When I saw him on my last visit to Rochester . . . I had been shocked to find him so near death. The giant he had once been was now shattered by the storms of life.

With the passing years had come to me better understanding of father, and mutual sympathy had drawn us gradually closer. . . . It was helped also by my awakening to the complexities of sex as a force dominating our feelings. I had learned to understand better my own turbulent nature, and my experiences had made me see what had been obscure to me so long in the character of my father. His violence and hardness had only been symptoms of an intensely sexual nature that had failed to find adequate expression.

My parents had been brought together in the traditional Jewish orthodox fashion, without love. They were mismated from the first. Mother had been left a widow at twenty-three, with two children, a little store her only earthly possession. Whatever love she had had died with the young man to whom she had been married at the age of fifteen. Father had brought into the match a fire of passionate youth. His wife was only one year his senior and radiantly beautiful. The impelling need of his nature drove him to her and made him more insistent in proportion as mother fought back his insatiable hunger. My coming had marked her fourth childbirth, each one nearly bringing her to the grave. I recalled some remarks I had heard her make when I was too young to understand their meaning. They illuminated much that had been dark to me and caused me to realize what a purgatory my parents' intimacy must have been for them both. No doubt they would have been shocked had anyone called to their attention the true source of the struggle between them and of father's uncontrollable temper. With the decline of health came also a lessening of his erotic vitality and a resultant psychic change. Father grew more mellow, patient and kindly. The affection he had rarely shown his own children he now lavished on those of my two sisters. When I once referred to the harsh methods he had used towards us, he assured me that it could not be true. The tenderness that had come into his nature blotted out even the remembrance of past severity. The best in him, formerly hidden by emotional stress, by the struggle for existence and years of physical suffering, came into its own at last. He now felt and gave

us a newly born affection, which in its turn awakened our love for
him.

EMMA GOLDMAN

Love of a husband for his wife

Tonight

An evening at home:
sitting in the house and looking
out of the window.
The wife sits in her chair embroidering
and sewing maybe.
I turn around and look at her: she is just sitting there
not doing anything,
holding idle in her hands
the needle, the scissors, and the cloth,
thinking of our life together, day after day,
each with its worries;
how when we have a talk, the important thing always
    goes unsaid;
and how you never can escape
the habitual and boring routine of daily life;
how every day gone is lost –
it will never come back, never,
and just like today, tomorrow will pass,
and whatever it was you lived for
has defeated you.
She is thinking like this
when hopefully, she looks at you
at the very moment you turn from the window
and look at her too; and in that glance
everything becomes absolutely clear.
So you get up,
go over to her, your own wife,
put a hand gently on her shoulder
and with the other smooth back her hair,
and want to say many loving things
but you can't.

You look out the window again,
the night dark, the stars bright,
and in your heart is peace.

ZISHA LANDAU

Love of a wife for her husband

We make real sacrifices when we try to understand the otherness of people we love. We have to offer up our prejudices and preconceptions. They are as substantial as the sheep and goats and cattle offered up by our ancestors in the Bible.

A Husband Returns from War

You say goodnight to your friends and know that tomorrow you will meet them again, sound and safe as you will be. It is not like that where your husband is. There are the comrades, closer in friendship to him than you can ever be, whom he has seen comic or wild or thoughtful; and then broken or dead. There are some who have gone out with a wave of the hand and a gay obscenity, and have never come back. We do not know such things; prefer, and wisely, to close our minds against them. . . .

I have been trying to say that women have the easier part in war. But when the war is over – then we must take up. The truth is that women's work begins when war ends, begins on the day their men come home to them. For who is that man, who will come back to you? You know him as he was; you have only to close your eyes to see him sharp and clear. You can hear his voice whenever there is silence. But what will he be, this stranger who comes back? How are you to throw a bridge across the gap that has separated you – and that is not the little gap of months and miles? He has seen the world aflame; he comes back to your new red dress. He has known glory and horror and filth and dignity; he will listen to you tell of the success of the canteen dance, the upholsterer who disappointed, the arthritis of your aunt. What have you to offer this man? . . . There have been people you never knew with whom he has had jokes you could not comprehend and talks that would be foreign to your ear. There are pictures hanging in his memory that he can never show you. Of this great part of his life, you have no share . . . things for ever out of your reach, far too many and too big for jealousy. That is where you start, and from there you go on to make a friend of that stranger from across a world.

DOROTHY PARKER

Illusions of love

The guy in the song probably believes his own words. We are not sure. Sex is instinctive and strong, and all nature uses camouflage to conceal and divert.

All I Really Want to Do

I ain't lookin' to compete with you,
Beat or cheat or mistreat you,
Simplify you, classify you,
Deny, defy or crucify you.
All I really want to do
Is, baby, be friends with you.

No, and I ain't lookin' to fight with you,
Frighten you or tighten you,
Drag you down or drain you down,
Chain you down or bring you down.
All I really want to do
Is, baby, be friends with you.

I ain't lookin' to block you up,
Shock or knock or lock you up,
Analyse you, categorize you,
Finalize you or advertise you.
All I really want to do
Is, baby, be friends with you.

I don't want to straight-face you,
Race or chase you, track or trace you,
Or disgrace you or displace you,
Or define you or confine you.
All I really want to do
Is, baby, be friends with you.

I don't want to meet your kin,
Make you spin or do you in,
Or select you or dissect you,
Or inspect you or reject you.
All I really want to do
Is, baby, be friends with you.

I don't want to fake you out,
Take or shake or forsake you out,
I ain't lookin' for you to feel like me,
See like me or be like me.
All I really want to do
Is, baby, be friends with you.

BOB DYLAN

The one who is incapable of love must learn how to flatter.

YIDDISH PROVERB

Perhaps this applies to prayers too!

Absolutely!

When the Spring comes in and the sun is bright
Then every small blossom beckons and blows.
When the moon on her shining journey goes
Then stars swim after her through the night.
When the singer looks into two clear eyes
Then something is stirred and lyrics arise. . . .
But flowers and stars and songs just begun,
And moonbeams and eyes and the light of the sun,
No matter how much such stuff may please,
One can't keep living on things like these.

HEINRICH HEINE

Memories of love

You have to live with a lot of guilt when you remember good people. How to use that guilt for good and not self-reproach! Or even worse, slip your guilt into someone else's pocket!

To My Mother

Other people say ordinary things
Like: "My mother used to spend hours
Unpicking string." Or:
"That trick of her old age
Nearly drove me to distraction."
I look at them
And try to comprehend
The simple action of remembering
Who have trained myself a childhood long
To forget so successfully.

What foibles were yours
That are now forgotten,
My mother? Only I spend time in wondering
Who do not recall even the contours
Of a face I must have scanned
A thousand times in fear and hope,
A face that is now the skin of a lamp
Lit in the darkness of some insomniac's night;
Mine perhaps. You say all this is corny,
Or "prurient". No doubt it is fashionable.

Yet I cannot forget
What I do not remember
Now that no one thinks of you at all
But I who cannot think
Not remembering how once
You must have been young and cheerful,
Once even silly and giggly going to school,
Sick or delayed or in love and glad,
Who lie now with the sod, still and anonymous,
Burnt or gassed. Other methods often worked too.

I must surely understand that agony
Was not the totality of your life,
Nor evil the unambiguous sum
Of your appalling going.

Then why should I who cannot remember
What you were nurse the residual wound
Of your mutilated absence
More than my neighbour who led you to die?
Must we all have atoned
For the crimes we are yet to commit?

HILDA SCHIFF

*You can learn a lot about religion, if you meditate on texts from a jukebox,
because it's the same love, whether it's directed to God or one of His
creatures.*

Our romance won't end on a sorrowful note,
　　Though by tomorrow you're gone;
The song is ended, but as the songwriter wrote,
　　"The melody lingers on."
　They may take you from me,
　　I'll miss your fond caress.
　But though they take you from me,
　　I'll still possess:

Refrain
　The way you wear your hat,
　　The way you sip your tea,
　The mem'ry of all that –
No, no! They can't take that away from me!

　The way your smile just beams,
　　The way you sing off key,
　The way you haunt my dreams –
No, no! They can't take that away from me!

　We may never, never meet again
　　On the bumpy road to love,
　Still I'll always, always keep
　　The mem'ry of –

The way you hold your knife,
    The way we danced till three,
    The way you've changed my life –
No, no! They can't take that away from me!
No! They can't take that away from me!

IRA GERSHWIN

6 · RELATIONSHIPS

Animals – calves, asses and small creatures

I don't think prophets, rabbis or apostles were partial to pets, but they tried to be considerate and kind. There is a nice dog in Tobit, but he has fallen between two stools, as it were, and ended up in the Apocrypha.

Rabbi Judah the Prince was sitting studying the Torah in front of the Babylonian synagogue in Sepphoris when a calf passed before him on its way to slaughter. It began to cry out as though saying: "Save me!" He replied: "What can I do for you? It is for this that you were fashioned." As a punishment he suffered toothache for thirteen years. . . . One day a creeping thing ran past his daughter who tried to kill it. He said: "My daughter, let it alone, for it is written: 'His mercies are over all His works'" (Psalm 145:9). At once he was restored to health.

Genesis Rabbah 33:3

Alexander the Great of Macedon visited King Katzia (a legendary African king) to see his way of conducting justice. A man came with a case against his neighbour. He said: "This man sold me a dunghill and I found a treasure in it." The buyer said: "I only bought a dunghill, not a treasure." The seller said: "I sold a dunghill and anything in it." The king said to one of them: "Do you have a son?" He replied: "Yes." He said to the other: "Do you have a daughter?" He replied: "Yes." So he said to them: "Let them marry each other and the treasure can belong to both of them."

He saw that Alexander was astonished and asked: "Have I not judged well?" He replied: "Yes." "If the case came before you, how would you have judged?" Alexander replied: "I would have killed both of them and kept the treasure for myself." The king asked him: "Does it rain in your country?" He answered: "Yes." He asked: "Does the sun shine?" He answered: "Yes." "Do you have small cattle?" Alexander replied: "Yes." Said the king: "Then it is clearly not for your sake that the rain falls and the sun shines but for their sake! As it says 'man and beast You preserve, O Lord' (Psalm 36:7). Read the verse instead as: 'man, for the sake of the beast, You preserve, O Lord!'"

Genesis Rabbah 33:1

Balaam arose in the morning, saddled his ass and went with the princes of Moab. Then God was angry that he went and an angel of the Lord stationed itself in the path to prevent him. Now he was riding on his ass and his two assistants were with him. When the ass saw the angel of the Lord positioned in the path with its sword drawn in its hand, the ass turned aside from the path and went into the field. But Balaam beat the ass to turn it back to the path. Then the angel of the Lord stood in a lane between the vineyards with a wall on either side. When the ass saw the angel of the Lord she pressed against the wall and crushed Balaam's foot against the wall, so he beat her again! Yet again the angel of the Lord moved and stood in a narrow place where there was no room to turn either right or left. The ass saw the angel of the Lord and lay down under Balaam. Then Balaam was furious and struck the ass with his staff. But the Lord opened the mouth of the ass and she said to Balaam: "What have I done to you that you should hit me these three times?" Balaam said to the ass: "Because you have made a mockery of me! If I had a sword in my hand now I'd kill you!" The ass said to Balaam: "Look, it's me, your ass on which you have been riding all along till this day. Have I been in the habit of doing this to you?" And he answered: "No."

Then the Lord opened Balaam's eyes and he saw the angel of the Lord stationed in the way with a drawn sword in its hand and he bowed and fell on his face.

Numbers 22:21–31

When I travel in my coach to teach Torah, give me thought for the mare that carries me, and guard her from my impatience; when I walk through Your woods, may my right foot and my left foot be harmless to the little creatures that move in the grasses; as it is

said by the mouth of Your prophet, They shall not hurt nor
destroy in all My holy mountain. Amen.

RABBI MOSHE HAKOTUN

Mothers in sentiment, spirit and sociology

*It's sentimental, but the self-sacrifice is real, for many middle-aged Jews
have known such women. The Yiddishe fathers, immersed in ritual, were
remote by comparison. Underneath the symbols of patriarchy, matri-
archy ruled.*

My Yiddishe Momma

Of things I should be thankful for I've had a goodly share
And as I sit in the comfort of a cosy chair
My fancy takes me to a humble East Side tenement
Three flights in the rear to where my childhood days were
    spent.
It wasn't much like paradise but amid the dirt and all
There sat the sweetest angel one that I fondly call
My yiddishe momma
I need her more than ever now.
My yiddishe momma
I'd love to kiss that wrinkled brow.
I long to hold her hands once more
As in days gone by
And ask her to forgive me for
Things I did that made her cry.
How few were her pleasures
She never cared for fashion styles.
Her jewels and treasures
She found them in her baby's smiles.
Oh I know that I owe what I am today
To that dear little lady so old and grey,
To that wonderful yiddishe momma,
Momma mine.

JACK YELLEN

Historically, cross-culturally, a woman's status as childbearer has
been the test of her womanhood. Through motherhood, every

woman has been defined from outside herself: mother, matri-
arch, matron, spinster, barren, old maid – listen to the history of
emotional timbre that hangs about each of these words. Even by
default motherhood has been an enforced identity for women,
while the phrases "childless man" and "nonfather" sound
absurd and irrelevant to us.

And so this woman in labour is on the one hand, even perhaps
in terror and pain, doing what history has told her it was her duty
and destiny to do; while at the same time doing what her mother
did, re-enacting a scene, which both separates her from her own
mother (for now she is, supposedly, herself a woman and no
longer a child) and creates her more intensely in her mother's
image.

ADRIENNE RICH

When your husband walks out on you

*In traditional Jewish law, it is difficult for deserted women to get a divorce
and remarry – impossible if the husband cannot be cajoled or coerced. The
injustice was (and sometimes is) still endured by traditional pious
women.*

A Poem of Women

Sometimes in the night the women of our family will
    come to me in dreams and say:
"We have modestly borne our pure blood over generations
And brought it to you like a vintage wine
From the Kosher wine cellars of our hearts."
And one of them will say:
"I was left a deserted wife
When my cheeks, two rosy apples,
Were still on the tree.
And I ground my white teeth
In the lonely nights of waiting."
And I shall comfort my grandmothers, saying:
"Your sighs, breathed like whips,
Have driven my young life from your house
From your pure beds I have fled.

But still you pursue me
Where streets lie in darkness
Where shadows appear
And your silent stifled cries
Prey upon me like chill harvest winds
And your words are silken cords
Binding my brain.
My life is a page torn from a holy book
And the first line smeared."

KADIA MOLODOVSKY

A father fighting to keep his pride

We hurried on, our heads bent against the wind, to the cluster of lights ahead that was 149th Street and Westchester Avenue, and those lights seemed to me the brightest lights I had ever seen. Tugging at my father's coat, I started down the line of pushcarts. There were all kinds of things that I wanted, but since nothing had been said by my father about buying a present, I would merely pause before a pushcart to say, with as much control as I could muster, "Look at that chemistry set!" or, "There's a stamp album!" or, "Look at the printing press!" Each time my father would pause and ask the pushcart man the price. Then without a word we would move on to the next pushcart. Once or twice he would pick up a toy of some kind and look at it and then at me, as if to suggest this might be something I might like, but I was ten years old and a good deal beyond just a toy; my heart was set on a chemistry set or a printing press. There they were on every pushcart we stopped at, but the price was always the same and soon I looked up and saw we were nearing the end of the line. Only two or three more pushcarts remained. My father looked up, too, and I heard him jingle some coins in his pocket. In a flash I knew it all. He'd gotten together about seventy-five cents to buy me a Christmas present, and he hadn't dared say so in case there was nothing to be had for so small a sum.

As I looked up at him I saw a look of despair and disappointment in his eyes that brought me closer to him than I had ever been in my life. I wanted to throw my arms around him and say, "It doesn't matter . . . I understand . . . this is better than a chemistry set or a printing press . . . I love you." But instead we stood shivering beside each other for a moment – then turned away from the last two pushcarts and started silently back home. I don't know why the words remained choked up within me. I didn't even take his hand on the way home nor did he take mine. We were not on that basis. Nor did I ever tell him how close to him I felt that night – that for a while the concrete wall between father and son had crumbled away and I knew that we were two lonely people struggling to reach each other.

MOSS HART

Children

The best security for old age: respect your children.

SHOLEM ASCH

God help all children as they move into a time of life they do not understand, and must struggle through with precepts they have picked from the garbage cans of older people, clinging with the passion of the lost to odds and ends that will mess them up for all time, or hating the trash so much they will waste their future on the hatred.

LILLIAN HELLMAN

One father supports ten children, but ten children do not support one father.

YIDDISH PROVERB

Simone Weil was born a Jewess but she disliked Judaism. Like other Jews she suffered for it however and never got baptized, though she tottered on the edge of the font. She is very irritating and very honest. I sometimes want to hurl her books through the window but pick them up instead, underlining whole sentences or writing rude and angry comments in the margins. There is no sentiment or flab in her writings, just the basics of belief, mixed with bits of prejudice as I've said. It's the real thing, but very hard to accept.

When a child in his play breaks something valuable, his mother does not love the breakage. But if later on her son goes far away or dies she thinks of the incident with infinite tenderness because she now sees it only as one of the signs of her child's existence. It is in this way that we ought to love God through everything good and everything evil, without distinction. If we love only through what is good, then it is not God we are loving but something earthly to which we give that name. We must not try to reduce evil to good by seeking compensations or justifications for evil. We must love God through the evil that occurs, solely because everything that actually occurs is real and behind all reality stands God.

SIMONE WEIL

When the kids were young

A lot is written about family life. Some of it seems very sacred but is very synthetic. This seems to be the real stuff.

I was the same kind of father as I was a harpist – I played by ear. But I've been lucky on both scores. The harp has given me a decent living and my children have given me more pleasure than I ever thought a man could possibly have.

What rules we had, as a family, stemmed from the fact that all of us had been adopted by each other. We've always had equal amounts of gratitude and respect mixed in with our love for each other. Susan, an only child who never had any roots, and I, a lone wolf who got married twenty years too late, were adopted by the kids as much as they were by us.

Somehow, without lecturing or threatening or studying any books, we all followed the same rules, from the time the kids were very young:

Life has been created for you to enjoy, but you won't enjoy it unless you pay for it with some good, hard work. This is one price that will never be marked down.

You can work at whatever you want to as long as you do it as well as you can and clean up afterwards and you're at the table at mealtime and in bed at bedtime.

Respect what the others do. Respect Dad's harp, Mom's paints, Billy's piano, Alex's set of tools, Jimmy's designs, and Minnie's menagerie.

If anything makes you sore, come out with it. Maybe the rest of us are itching for a fight too.

If anything strikes you as funny, out with that too. Let's all the rest of us have a laugh.

If you have an impulse to do something you're not sure is right, go ahead and do it. Take a chance. Chances are, if you don't you'll regret it – unless you break the rules about mealtime or bedtime, in which case you'll sure as hell regret it.

If it's a question of whether to do what's fun or what is supposed to be good for you, and nobody is hurt by whichever you do, always do what's fun.

If things get too much for you and you feel the whole world's against you, go stand on your head. If you can think of anything crazier to do, do it.

Don't worry about what other people think. The only person in the world important enough to conform to is yourself.

Anybody who mistreats a pet or breaks a pool cue is docked a month's pay.

HARPO MARX

7 · CHALLENGES

Breakdown

> For man
> is in this world as in a
> ship that is crossing the
> great ocean and seems
> to be breaking apart.
>
> *Zohar*

So long as the world moves along accustomed paths, so long as there are no wild catastrophes, man can find sufficient substance for his life by contemplating surface events, theories and movements of society. He can acquire his inner richnesses from this external kind of "property". But this is not the case when life encounters fiery forces of evil and chaos. Then the "revealed" world begins to totter. Then the man who tries to sustain himself only from the surface aspects of existence will suffer terrible impoverishment, begin to stagger . . . then he will feel welling up within himself a burning thirst for that inner substance and vision which transcends the obvious surfaces of existence and remains unaffected by the world's catastrophes. From such inner sources he will seek the waters of joy which can quicken the dry outer skeleton of existence.

RAV KOOK

Facing the music

I don't despise the humble heroism of people who try to carry on doing small, sane, normal things in insecure times. In 1936 Hitler was at the high point of success.

> O, Lord, God of Abraham!
> Forgive me my sins!
> Do not turn away from me with
>   your sharp command!
> I must dance now!
> For is there anyone in the world
> Who lives, when Death does not
>   wish it?
> Don Rabbi with the long beard,
> You have always studied Talmud
>   and the Holy Writ,
> And sought the truth in the world!
> Dance, then, and do not regret it!
> Sing, then, and may your blessing be
>   turned into song!
> And then you can rest together with
>   Ashi.
>
> MEDIAEVAL YIDDISH SONG

Courage

Ministers are travelling salesmen but we cannot sell security, though that's what people want. It is not on offer – only courage.

> When your life is tumbling downhill head over heels,
> Thrashing and foaming like an epileptic,
> Don't pray and offer up repentance,
> Don't be afraid of jail and ruin.

Study your past with concentration,
Evaluate your days without self-flattery,
Grind the fag-ends of illusions underfoot,
But open up to all that's bright and clear.

Don't surrender to impotence and bitterness,
Don't give in to disbelief and lies,
Not everyone's a cringing bastard,
Not everyone's a bigot who informs.

And while you walk along the alien roads
To lands which do not figure on your maps,
Count out the names of all your friends
As you would do with pearls or prayer-beads.

Be on the look-out, cheerful and ferocious,
And you'll manage to stand up, yes, stand up
Under your many layered load of misery,
Under the burden of your being right.

YULI DANIEL (written in a labour camp)

Middle age

Life Begins at Forty

I've often heard it said and sung
That life is sweetest when you're young
And kids sixteen to twenty-one
Think they're having all the fun.
I disagree, I say it isn't so
And I'm one gal who ought to know.
I started young and I'm still going strong
But I've learned as I've gone along
That life begins at forty
That's when love and living start
To become a gentle art.
A woman who's been careful finds
That's when she's in her prime
And a good man when he's forty knows
Just how to take his time.

Conservative or sporty,
It's not until you're forty
That you learn the how and why
And the what and when.

In the twenties and the thirties
You want your love in large amounts
But after you reach forty
It's the quality that counts.
Yes, life begins at forty
And I've just begun to live all over again.
You see, the sweetest things in life
Grow sweeter as the years roll on
Like the music from a violin
That has been well played upon,
And the sweetest smoke
Is from a mellow broken-in old pipe
And the sweetest-tasting peach is one
That's *zaftig*, round and ripe.

In the twenties and the thirties
You're just an amateur
But after you reach forty
That's when you become a connoisseur.
Then it isn't grab and get it
And a straight line for the door.
You're not hasty, you're tasty,
You enjoy things so much more.

JACK YELLEN
(A Sophie Tucker monologue)

Midlife crisis

Why do we so object to growing older? Not just because we are approaching death, not even because we are conscious of failing powers. We mourn the passing years, unless we are among the happy few who have really understood their meaning, because with every one that passes we have left more undone and have less time to do it. Worse; we have left more undone and are less able to believe that we ever shall do it. But what is "it"? The writer has not yet produced a novel better than *War and Peace*; the composer, a symphony better than the Fifth; the childless woman, children; the politician, anything to secure lasting reputation; the aimless, a goal; the frightened, courage; the unhappy, happiness. But these are all only disguises for the truth, substitutes for the only true creation any of us can really achieve. Of what use the statesman's treaty, the painter's masterpiece, the general's victory, even the gardener's living tree? In the end, it is our own wholeness we must seek, and our only possible creation is ourselves; it is the realization that we have not yet achieved it, indeed that we have hardly begun on it, that brings the sound of time's wingèd chariot hurrying near. In this truth, Beethoven and Tolstoy are one with the barren woman, the failed husband, those who are afraid to die though they have never been alive. Is there a reckoning that awaits us all? I do not know; but there may be a terrible understanding *in articulo mortis* more painful than the torments of the damned. It is later than we think.

BERNARD LEVIN

Middle age . . . is when you pay for what you didn't have or couldn't do when you were young.

BERNARD MALAMUD

There are all sorts of flight from responsibility: There is flight into death, flight into sickness, and finally flight into folly. The last is the least dangerous and most convenient; and even to the wise, the way to it is usually not as far as they like to imagine.

ARTHUR SCHNITZLER

Though no specific sin or sins of the past come to mind, someone may feel that he is greatly pained, that he is filled with iniquity, that the light of God does not shine upon him. There is no "willing spirit" within him; his heart is calloused; his soul's qualities and characteristics do not go along the straight and desired way that leads to fulfilment of life . . . his conceptions are coarse and his emotions are a confusion of darkness and lust which causes him spiritual revulsion. He is ashamed of himself and he is aware that God is not within him, and this is his great anguish, his most frightful sin. He is embittered at himself and finds no escape from the snare of his pursuers, which has no specific nature, but he is at once taken completely captive. From this spiritual bitterness repentance emerges as healing by a skilful physician. The sensing of repentance and a deep knowledge of it . . . comes and streams into the soul.

RAV KOOK

Living with oneself

Blessed are You, Lord our God, king of the universe, who has made me as He wanted me.

Siddur

What is it that troubles you? Death? – Who lives for ever?
Or because your foot has stumbled on the earth? There is no man who has never stumbled.

SHMUEL HANAGID

He who in his life has never made a fool of himself has also never been wise.

HEINRICH HEINE

Nothing comes to man except by the decree of the Holy One, blessed be He. One should pray for God's mercy that whatever is decreed shall turn out for the sake of heaven.

Sefer Chasidim

This advice rings true but is beyond me, like a lot of religious advice.

Nostalgia

You get less moralistic when you remember.

My child, we two were children,
　　Two children, small and gay;
We used to creep to the hen-house
　　And hide beneath the hay.

We tried to chirp like chickens,
　　And hoped the passers-by
Would hear us there and fancy
　　They heard a chicken cry.

We built a lordly castle
　　With boxes, in the court,
And set up house together,
　　Quite grandly as we thought.

The old cat paid us visits
　　As often as she could;
We used to bow and curtsy
　　And "hoped her health was good".

We made her pretty speeches,
　　And spoke of this and that –
Things we have since repeated
　　To many a grave old cat.

We sat and talked as wisely
　　As grown-up people may;
Complaining things had altered
　　Most sadly since our day.

"Love, faith, and truth no longer
　　Existed anywhere:
But coffee had grown dearer
　　And money very rare!"

Those days are past, and all things
　　Are passing by, in sooth:
Money, the world, the ages,
　　And love and faith and truth.

                    HEINRICH HEINE

For our Jewish life devastated,
I pray to You, oh God!
I weep for Mother Vilna,
For Kolomeo and for Brod.

For Warsaw, Kovno, Kalish, Lemberg,
For towns both great and small
That have fallen to the conqueror,
Or still await their fall.

For every dirty Jewish alley,
I am grief-stricken, desolate.
For every drinking-bar and pawnshop,
And for our false measure and weight.

For every Jewish brothel
That stood in a non-Jewish town,
For all that once was ours,
And now has been burnt down.

They are all so lovely, things Jewish!
Our impoverished life rebuild!
And speak the word that is wanting,
That our anguish may be stilled!

ZISHA LANDAU

Suicidal

Résumé

Razors pain you;
Rivers are damp;
Acids stain you;
And drugs cause cramp.
Guns aren't lawful;
Nooses give;
Gas smells awful;
You might as well live.

DOROTHY PARKER

There is a chasidic story of a disciple who came to his Rebbe for help. He was desperate. His world was falling apart and he had no idea where to turn. "You must help me, Rebbe", he exclaimed. "You are my only hope." The Rebbe turned his soulful eyes on him and replied, "I cannot help you out of the thicket, my son, for I too am irrevocably caught up within it, but if you will come with me, I can at least lead you further into the thicket." There is a stage at which confusion and the inability to cope with the world is desperately painful and intolerable. But there is a further stage in which this state becomes transfigured and is no longer experienced as a problem but rather as the way that God set it all up and thus as a trip to be experienced and exalted as opposed to one which is to be seen as pathological and troubled.

MARK COHEN

When Hell happens

When the world gives way from under you, these survivors' tales might prove more relevant than you care to contemplate. The bottom can drop out of your world, as you motor home from work. It doesn't need anything as dramatic as a concentration camp! It is frightening as well as ennobling to think of what humans are capable of enduring and do.

There is no area of our existence in which fate has not cut its furrows deeply into our lives. We are not speaking of the disappearance of external prestige, nor of the separation from habitual and much loved activities which forced many to begin a new existence. Rather we feel that we, as no generation in many an age, confront our fate nakedly. The ground on which our feet stand is shaken, and for most of us it is still uncertain in which part of the earth we might find a new foothold. No wonder that many a one is seized by the fear that life is playing an incomprehensible game with him, and in his confusion he himself begins to think little of his life. But beyond all this is the worst: the inner anxiety which has grasped many of our people today, that fear of tomorrow which makes it impossible to bear the today. Like millstones, the same cares and thoughts turn again and again in his mind, shattering his nerves, destroying his powers. It seems as if the worst curse which the Bible expresses is to be fulfilled: "In the morning you shall say: 'if only it were evening', and in the evening 'if only it were morning!' " . . .

We stand naked before our fate, but thereby we are not only without the many things which formerly assisted us, but we are freed also of the ballast of prejudice, of the habits and conventions which narrowed our field of vision. We want to face reality, but we also do not want to give ourselves over to a fatalism which releases us from all obligations. We want to love our life because of, not despite, the fact that it has revealed itself to us in all its elemental power.

With such sentiments we prepare ourselves for the High Holydays of our year.

> *Der Morgen* (One of the last articles published
> in a Jewish magazine in Germany shortly
> before the Second World War)

It is a unique sound. A cell door has no handle, either outside or inside; it cannot be shut except by being slammed to. It is made of massive steel and concrete, about four inches thick, and every time it falls to there is a resounding crash as though a shot had been fired. But this report dies away without an echo. Prison sounds are echoless and bleak.

When the door has been slammed behind him for the first time, the prisoner stands in the middle of the cell and looks round. I fancy that everyone must behave in more or less the same way.

First of all he gives a fleeting look round the walls and takes a mental inventory of the objects in what is now to be his domain:

> the iron bedstead,
> the wash-basin,
> the WC,
> the barred window.

His next action is invariably to try to pull himself up by the iron bars of the window and look out. He fails, and his suit is covered with white from the plaster on the wall against which he has pressed himself. He desists, but resolves to practise and master the art of pulling himself up by his hands. He makes some more laudable resolutions; he will do exercises every morning; and learn a foreign language; and he simply won't let his spirit be broken. He dusts his suit and continues his voyage of exploration round his realm – five paces long by four paces broad. He tries the iron bedstead. The springs are broken, the wire mattress sags and cuts into the flesh; it's like lying in a hammock made of steel wire. He pulls a humorous face, being determined to prove to himself that he is full of courage and confidence. Then his gaze rests on the cell door, and he sees that an eye is glued to the spyhole and is watching him.

The eye goggles at him glassily, its pupil unbelievably large; it is an eye without a man attached to it, and for a few moments the prisoner's heart stops beating.

The eye disappears and the prisoner takes a deep breath and presses his hand against the left side of his chest.

"Now, then," he says to himself encouragingly, "how silly to go and get so frightened. You must get used to that: after all, the official's only doing his duty by peeping in; that's part of being in prison. But they won't get me down, they'll never get me down; I'll stuff paper in the spy-hole at night. . . ."

As a matter of fact there's no reason why he shouldn't do so straight away. The idea fills him with genuine enthusiasm. For the first time he experiences that almost manic desire for activity that from now on will alternate continually – up and down in a never-ending zig-zag – with apathy and depression.

Then he realizes that he has no paper on him, and his next impulse is – according to his social status – either to ring or to run over to the stationer's at the corner. This impulse lasts only the fraction of a second; the next moment he becomes conscious for the first time of the true significance of his situation. For the first time he grasps the full reality of being behind a door which is locked from outside, grasps it in all its searing, devastating poignancy.

This, too, lasts only a few seconds. The next moment the anaesthetizing mechanism gets going again, and brings about that merciful state of semi-narcosis induced by pacing up and down, forging plans, weaving illusions.

"Let's see," says the novice, "where were we? Ah, yes, that business of stuffing paper into the spy-hole. It *must* be possible to get hold of paper somehow." He leaves the "how" in this "somehow" suspended in mid-air. This is a mode of thought that he will soon master – or, rather, it will master him. "When I get out," he will say, for example, "I shall never worry about money again. I shall rub along somehow or other." Or: "When I get out, I shall never quarrel with the wife again. We'll manage to get along somehow."

Indeed, "somehow" everything will be all right once he's free. This stereotyped line of thought means that the outside world increasingly loses its reality for him; it becomes a vague dream world, a lost paradise in which everything is somehow possible.

"Where were we? . . . Oh, yes, that business of stuffing paper into the spyhole." Of course, somehow one can get hold of paper. But is it allowed? No, it's certain not to be allowed. So why bother? . . .

"Let's take a more thorough inventory of the objects in the room. Why, look, there's an iron table with a chair which we haven't observed or fully appreciated yet. Of course the chair can't be moved from the table: it's welded to it. A pity, otherwise one might use it as a bed table and put one's things on it when getting undressed – pocket-book, handkerchief, cigarettes, matches and so on. . . ."

Then it occurs to him that he has neither pocket-book nor handkerchief, cigarettes nor matches in his pocket.

The barometer of his mood falls a second time.

It rises again the moment he has tried the tap over the wash-basin. "Look, there's running water in prison – it isn't half as bad as one imagined from outside. After all there is a bed (and it's much healthier to sleep on a hard bed), a wash-basin, a table, a chair – what more does a man need? One must learn to live simply and unassumingly: a few exercises, reading, writing, learning a foreign language. . . ."

The next voyage of discovery is in the direction of the water closet. "Why, there's even one of these – it's really not half so bad." He pulls the plug. The chain refuses to function. And the barometer falls afresh.

It rises again once the subtle plan has been conceived of filling the bucket with water from the tap and of flushing the lavatory pan in this way. It falls again when it transpires that the tap has also ceased to function. It rises again when he reflects that there must be certain times of the day when the water runs. It falls – it rises – it falls – it rises. And this is how things are to go on – in the coming minutes, hours, days, weeks, years.

How long has he already been in the cell?

He looks at his watch: exactly three minutes.

ARTHUR KOESTLER

Exile

I have lost *everything*. . . . I have lost my native land; do you know what that means for a poet? . . . I have lost the cities where I worked and where I made an impression for a whole lifespan . . . . I have had to become my own world, my own mental space, the cradle of words.

KARL WOLFSKEHL (From a letter to a friend after fourteen years in exile from Germany)

The pogroms in Russia at the turn of this century caused widespread migration, and a certain rabbi found himself roaming all over Europe, looking for a new post. Finally he crossed to New York, and there, after months of correspondence, he was informed of an opening in Argentina. When a friend tried to dissuade him from going, saying Argentina was too far away, the wanderer sighed: "Too far away? From where?"

The Wisdom of Israel

Rabbi Chenoch of Alexander once said: The real exile of Israel in Egypt was that they learned to endure it.

Chasidic

Said the Belzer: There are three kinds of exile: exile among the nations; exile among Jews; and exile among one's own desires . . . . The worst exile is the exile from peace of mind. It is suffered by one who is overpowered by his evil desires at the same time that he is aware of their wickedness. The last-named needs redemption most urgently.

Chasidic

The price of survival

But as a survivor myself I can at least testify that most of those who have survived went through that "universe" (the concentration camp "universe") with withdrawn antennae, divorced from truth, from reality, from normal human and humane values, substituting those with a different code and rituals, which now may look crazy or perverted; the choice, in order to survive, was: losing one's humanity or inventing a new one, losing one's dignity or inventing new symbols to keep it. One went on by forgetting immediately what had been done to one or what one had done the day before, thus being able to face the next blow.

For many, all that was left of their human countenance was a feeling of shame for being able to suffer what others were not; to survive what others did not; and be tormented by an eternal question – did one outlive the others because one was less sensitive, or even worse, did one live in some way at the expense of the death of others? There is hardly a survivor, articulate or not, who does not feel persecuted and accused by his dead companions, or who in the deepest chamber of his soul does not feel his own staying alive *vis-à-vis* dying, as only temporary reprieve. In that sense, one has not at all rejoined the world of the living; one is here merely waiting for the final call.

VERA ELYASHIV

Anyone who cannot cope with life while he is alive needs one hand to ward off a little his despair over his fate . . . but with his other hand he can jot down what he sees among the ruins, for he sees different and more things than the others; after all, he is dead in his own lifetime and the real survivor.

FRANZ KAFKA

Taking stock – sorting out the debris in drawers and in us

He sorted out the muddle in the loft
And left confusion running round his head instead.
He'd always meant to go up in the loft
And sort out the boxes crammed with

Things so necessary to life
He'd not missed for years.
It's amazing what we learn to live
Without
Or really never need.
So many things to look through,
Why does he feel so sad?
Throwing away things he doesn't use
Or forgot he ever had.
Is it just the passing of the years,
Or is it what he could or should have done
He fears?
Can we hope to live a life
So full
That the future is the goal,
Or do most of us look nostalgically back
And never see the whole?
Perhaps it's best to leave no trace
Of what took place before,
But to hoard one's past
Is so secure
As we don't know what's in store.
So, he sorted out his past in the loft
And left confusion running around his head instead.

ETHNE FREEMAN

I did great things. I built myself mansions and planted vineyards.
I laid out gardens and parks, planting every kind of fruit tree in
them. I had pools made to water a forest of trees. I bought slaves,
male and female, though I had a large household; herds and
flocks I owned, more than anyone before me in Jerusalem. I
amassed silver and gold, the treasure of kings and provinces.
Singers both male and female were mine, all the delights of men,
mistresses beyond number. So I grew great, greater than anyone
before me in Jerusalem, and my wisdom remained with me. I
denied my eyes nothing they desired, refused my heart no
pleasure – for my heart rejoiced in all my labour, and that was my
reward for all my labour. Then I took a long look at all my hands
had achieved, at all the effort I had put into its achieving – and all

of it was vanity and chasing the wind; nothing really gained under the sun.

Ecclesiastes 2:4–11

Ten enemies cannot do a man the harm that he does to himself.

YIDDISH PROVERB

Hanging on

A woman who lived next door to Rabbi Moshe Leib lost one child after another before they were a year old. Once when she was in the zaddik's house, she cried aloud: "A God who gives you children just to take them away again is not good: he is a cruel God!" Rabbi Leib's wife scolded her: "That's no way to talk! What you should say is: 'We cannot fathom God's mercy, and what He does is well done.'"

"Oh, no!" said the rabbi, who heard them talking from where he sat in his room and came out to join them. "You must not be resigned. Take courage, woman, and take strength. A year from now you will have a son: and in time to come I shall lead him under the bridal canopy." And so it was.

MARTIN BUBER

To you that build the new house

"There are stones like souls."

(RABBI NACHMAN)

When you come to put up your walls anew –
Your stove, your bedstead, table and chair –
Do not hang your tears for those who departed,
Who will not live with you then,
On to the stone.
Nor on the timber –
Else weeping will pierce the sleep,
The brief sleep you have yet to take.

Do not sigh when you bed your sheets,
Else your dreams will mingle
With the sweat of the dead.

Oh, the walls and household utensils
Are responsive as Aeolian harps
Or like a field in which your sorrow grows,
And they sense your kinship with dust.

Build, when the hourglass trickles,
But do not weep away the minutes
Together with the dust
That obscures the light.

NELLY SACHS

8 · PROSPECTS

Old Age – "The evil days?"

Remember also your creator in the days of your youth before the evil days come and the years arrive when you say: "I have no pleasure in them"; before the sun and the light and the moon and the stars are darkened and the clouds return after the rain; in the day when the keepers of the house tremble and the strong men are bent and the grinders cease because they are few, and those who look through the windows are dimmed, and the doors to the street are shut; when the sound of the grinding is low, and one rises at the sound of a bird and all the daughters of song are brought low; they are afraid too of heights and there are terrors on the road. The almond tree may blossom, the grasshopper drag itself along and the caper bush bud again, but man goes to his eternal home and the mourners go about the streets. Before the silver cord is snapped, or the golden bowl is broken, or the pitcher is broken at the fountain, or the wheel broken at the cistern, and the dust returns to the earth as it was, and the spirit returns to God who gave it.

Ecclesiastes 12:1–7

I shake and tremble as I rise from sitting down. I walk unsteadily till I get into my stride. I hunch and my head hangs forward, in short my body behaves like everyone else's who has grown old. Yet I never expected it would come to that. That I should submit to the average – never, never! And is my mind as doddering as my body? I cannot believe it, although I know how shrunk my horizon is, how restricted my present range of impersonal interests, how disinclined it is to make an effort. All the same I have the feeling that as an instrument it is as good as ever. And if not, then are the youngs – *les jeunes* – right in ignoring me altogether, or taking my pronouncements as symptoms of advanced senility? That I should come to that – I, son of the morning who had the animal conviction that he could never get senile no matter how old he got. One does not escape the law of averages.

BERNARD BERENSON, 7th November 1953, aged 89

Your body breaks down as you get older – like your car or your freezer. But as the outer shell wears thin, sometimes an inner light shows up more clearly – as in Rembrandt's portraits of old people. It is not all loss! There is release from expectation – other people's and your own – and you learn to bully yourself less.

Our lives can reach seventy years,
    eighty years with strength,
and they are troubled with grief and emptiness,
    but this is soon over and then we move on.

Psalm 90:10

In the country of the old and sick there are environmental hazards. Cautious days. Early nights. A silent, ageing life in which the anxiety of the invalid overrides the vitality of the untouched. A wariness, in case the untoward might go undetected. Sudden gratitude that turns bitterness into self-reproach.

ANITA BROOKNER

According to all the standards we employ . . . the aged person is condemned as inferior. . . . Conditioned to operating as a machine for making and spending money, with all other relationships dependent upon its efficiency, the moment the machine is out of order and beyond repair, one begins to feel like a ghost without a sense of reality. . . . Regarding himself as a person who has outlived his usefulness, he feels as if he has to apologize for being alive.

May I suggest that man's potential for change and growth is much greater than we are willing to admit, and that old age be regarded not as the age of stagnation but as *the age of opportunities for inner growth*.

The years of old age . . . are indeed formative years, rich in possibilities to unlearn the follies of a lifetime, to see through inbred self-deceptions, to deepen understanding and compassion, to widen the horizon of honesty, to refine the sense of fairness.

ABRAHAM JOSHUA HESCHEL

> When you are old, I am still the same,
> and when your hair turns grey, I will support you;
> I have made and I will bear,
> I will support and I will save.

Isaiah 46:4

Illness

Heal us, Lord, and we shall be healed, save us, and we shall be saved, for it is You we praise. Send relief and healing for all our diseases, our sufferings and our wounds, for You are a merciful and faithful healer. Blessed are You Lord, who heals the sick.

Siddur

Two men, let us suppose, are both affected with a chronic and always dangerous disease. One makes that circumstance the focal point of his thought and feeling. He knows all along that he has in himself elements of health, that his life situation is still enjoyable and worthwhile. His illness, however, looms most prominently in his spiritual landscape and, so, absorbs his first thought and effort. The other is fully aware of his ailment. He recognizes that he dare not forget it for an instant, or live even most fleetingly in violation of the restraints it imposes, or cease ever to hedge it in. Yet for him the most conspicuous feature of his being is not this, grave as it is. He is, therefore, likely to get along better as patient to his physician, as labourer, as kinsman, as citizen, certainly as a companion to others who, in like case with him, travel the road by his side. . . .

MILTON STEINBERG

Suffering

A man who was afflicted with a terrible disease complained to Rabbi Israel of Rizhyn that his suffering interfered with his learning and praying. The rabbi put his hand on his shoulder and said: "How do you know, friend, what is more pleasing to God, your studying or your suffering?"

MARTIN BUBER

Making a will

Impending death and the process of dying are still secret. They're not even real secrets, they're pretend secrets. Everyone knows, but everyone pretends that the others are in ignorance, so it can't be talked about or discussed, or brought into the open. All this is very often to the detriment of the dying, as well as those who care for them. The pretence and lying undermine the trust and care when it's needed most.

An elderly couple many years ago received a circular from the Federation of Synagogues asking if they wanted to reserve places in the cemetery at Edmonton, which was fast filling up. They tore the letter into little shreds, as though by eliminating the letter, they could eliminate death, and their large family now trudge annually to Rainham.

An old aunt took any discussion of death or making a will as a personal insult and proof of her family's wish to get rid of her as soon as possible. She was convinced that making a will would be a sign to the Almighty that she was ready to go. The consequence was unseemly squabbling after her death, because she had not made her wishes known.

But although we laugh at other people's superstitions, deep down most of us are reluctant to make wills, only rushing out to get the form or contacting a solicitor when we're suddenly faced with surgery. . . .

But I've seen many people coping tranquilly with their own impending death. They've not been superhuman, but ordinary people who have found comfort in being able to bring their lives to a close, and live out the last of their days and months being able to talk to those they love about how life would be without them. It may sound extraordinary and perhaps those people are unusual in having faith in themselves and the people around them, or a strong, religious faith. But faith itself is an unknown quality. It's a bit like jumping into the water and not being certain whether you can swim or not. When they do, most people stay afloat. The real problem is that we sometimes don't get the chance to jump, but get pushed. On the whole, I believe that faith is a risk worth taking. Otherwise you might get left with deathbed instructions, like the old man who, on dying, wanted his wife to promise him that she would drive to the cemetery in the same car as his sister whom she detested. Reluctantly, she agreed. "All right," she said, "I'll do it, but it will completely spoil my day."

Dying nearly always spoils the day; the important thing is that death doesn't destroy the living, and that they are not left with too many regrets and too many things that were left unsaid.

WENDY GREENGROSS

Every man knows that he must die, but no one believes it.

YIDDISH PROVERB

A wealthy man was being laid to rest, and his relatives followed the bier with loud lamentations. Motke Habad, happening to see the cortège, joined the mourners and started weeping even more demonstratively than the rest.

"Are you too a relative of the deceased?" he was asked.

He shook his head, but continued weeping.

"Then why all your grief?"

"That's the reason", he replied.

The Wisdom of Israel

Shrouds have no pockets.

YIDDISH PROVERB

In the hospital

Even if you've been visiting hospitals for forty years, you still don't know what to say in them. It helps both the visitor and the visited if they can hold hands. The patients are patient and try to put ministers at their ease.

Letter

I hope he doesn't see me walking past
   his bed
but if he does, I'll make believe
I didn't hear him if he calls.

Young man, a minute please.
I can't get out of it I guess.
I don't mind the time, it's the smell
of old age and rotting flesh I hate.

I want to talk to you.
He'll tell me what a mighty man he
   was.
I'll bet he's pressed a million pants,
and even was a Socialist
before his kidneys took up all his time.

Come closer please, I want to ask you
   if you have some time to spare.
I've got the time all right
but not enough to sing, to love, to go
   away
and never to see that ugly face again.

To write for me a letter for my wife.
Was she tall was she short was she fat
was she thin when it mattered what
   she was?
Are there any more at home like him?

And tell her this, but say it in your own
   words;
Never in my own words
I've got a sacred language
that she wouldn't understand.

Dear Rose;
Tonight I feel so bad I want to die.
That's not the way I feel tonight,
Dear Jane; That's not the way I feel
   at all.
Dear God that's not the way.

Please try to come and don't be mad
  no more.
I didn't see you now a long time.
In my own words, if she remembers
anything that wasn't groaning,
  slobbering,
unclean, she'd never come.

And bring the boy. I want to talk to you
  before I die.
What can the old man have to say
that must be said to them, to me
or anyone alive? What?

Love,
Abraham

ALEXANDER BERGMAN

Everyone feels the existence of evil and feels horror at it and
wants to get free from it. Evil is neither suffering nor sin; it is both
at the same time, it is something common to them both. For they
are linked together; sin makes us suffer and suffering makes us
evil, and this indissoluble complex of suffering and sin is the evil
in which we are submerged against our will, and to our horror.

A part of the evil that is within us we project into the objects of
our attention and desire; and they reflect it back to us, as if the evil
came from them. It is for this reason that any place where we find
ourselves submerged in evil inspires us with hatred and disgust.
It seems to us that the place itself is imprisoning us in evil. Thus
an invalid comes to hate his room and the people around him,
even if they are dear to him; and workers sometimes hate their
factory, and so on.

SIMONE WEIL

In Order to Drive Him Mad

In order to drive him mad
put him in a bed
in a ward
in a hospital
and let him know he's ill.

Not how ill
or what illness,
merely suggest it is
very, very grave.

Test blood, urine, sputum, X-Rays
but always be awaiting one more
key result.

Discuss him at the foot of the bed
in whispers
in loud erudition
with worried frown
with anecdotes
with laughter
that he cannot share.

Establish about him an air
of urgency
efficiency
into which, apologetic
he must intrude
his trivial pain.

Drug him at night
by day
give each injection, pill
its own mystique
and timing
and importance.
Then one day
quite without warning
change it.

Surround him with noise, activity
remove all privacy
make sure at least one patient
in a nearby bed
expires
and let him learn and fear those signs
of awkwardness
embarrassed glance
that mark the next to go.

If all these measures fail
as time goes by
and interest in him
slides away
suggest he goes back home
relaxes for a while
no overwork or strain
just takes it easy
returns for blood tests now and then
and with a final, hesitant frown
bid him
adieu.

JONATHAN MAGONET

Terminal illness

Lord, do Thou guide me on my pilgrim way,
Then shall I be at peace, whate'er betide me;
The morn is dark, the clouds hang low and grey,
Lord, do Thou guide me.

Let not the mists of sin from Thee divide me,
But pierce their gloom with mercy's golden ray,
Then shall I know that Thou in love hast tried me.

O'er rugged paths be Thou my staff and stay,
Beneath Thy wings from storm and tempest hide me,
Through life to death, through death to heavenly day
Lord, do Thou guide me.

ALICE LUCAS

Her statements sound trite and the style and sentiment are dated, but you find yourself repeating her lines while waiting for God-knows-what in a waiting room in Harley Street.

Waiting Rooms

Heavy curtains in the waiting rooms
of famous doctors drape the windows like a pall;
no distant murmur of men ascends to them,
no rattle of wagons from the street below.

Around the room pictures of long ago
gaze darkly; statues freeze before they spring.
Deep is the red of cupboard and of wall;
an ancient silence covers everything.

A man drowns in these heavy silences,
lost in the chair's upholstery, a light put out,
an object like the objects all about.

But when on the softness of rugs a step draws near,
a shiver goes through him, shakes him out of his ease.
He stares at the doctor with great bulging eyes.

DAVID VOGEL

The life of man means more than the narrowness of existence in
this world. With all its deficiencies and limitations, its pain and
suffering, it is, as the old Rabbinic metaphor says, but a place of
"preparation", an "ante-chamber"; it is only the "life of the
hour". The true life is the "eternal life". Man is created and
destined to be different from the world, to be holy. As the image
of God he belongs to that other, the higher life; he is a "child of the
world to come".

LEO BAECK

In her last sickness, my mother took my hand in hers
tightly: for the first time I knew
how calloused a hand it was, and how soft was mine.

CHARLES REZNIKOFF

Dying

*Traditional religion delights in deathbed testimonies and conversions.
Indeed every religious tradition has its stories of martyrs who are
surprisingly loquacious, considering their situation. They are edifying,
of course, but you can also get a lot from people whom death doesn't seem
to alter. As Voltaire lay dying, his curtains were set alight by a candle.
"Déjà les flammes", he commented, which was courageous in the
circumstances.*

I remember two meetings with ladies who were dying.

The first began with a phone call late one Friday night. The hospital said a Jewish woman was dying and wanted to see a Rabbi straight away; tomorrow might be too late. So I arrived around midnight, clutching a prayerbook. (Actually I clutched two prayerbooks, one Reform and one Orthodox, just in case.)

She said: "Rabbi, they tell me I am dying, and I want you to make sure that my daughter does not get my mink coat."

Stunned, I tried to grope for some deeper significance to our conversation, while she continued with her catalogue of jewels, watches and other precious items, which she apportioned in order to spite her daughter. At last, I said in exasperation: "Madam, you don't want a Rabbi. You want a lawyer!"

"I know," she said, "but no lawyer would come out at this time of night."

It was a cheerful misuse of religion. After I refused to re-draw her will, we had a short pleasant discussion about her childhood, her youth and her dancing days. She survived till the following day and, after seeing her lawyer, she died.

I spent some time with her family and it seems that she had always seen property and people as symbols of power. She had died still attached to her petty possessions and quarrels, leaving behind an inheritance of bitterness.

Another hospital phoned. A lady was dying and would not survive more than a day or two. "Does she know?" I asked. "We have not told her", they said to me.

I entered the room wondering how to start the conversation. She began: "Rabbi, I am dying."

She was utterly miserable, because in her eyes her great sins made her unfit to be in the presence of God. She had never given much thought to God, and her so-called crimes were largely ancient matters to do with her family. I suggested that she might talk to her family and to God, and ask their forgiveness. This seemed to come to her as a revelation.

To the hospital's surprise she lasted three more weeks. She spent the time talking to her family – physically to those who were alive and visiting her, and mentally to those who had died. She also made her peace with God.

It was a privilege to watch her and the family as they worked together. They all seemed to grow, to become more alive. When she died she was at peace. In her death she had become fully alive. Those three weeks have remained a precious source of wonder for her family and for me. It is so rare for a Rabbi to feel really useful.

DANIEL SMITH

My mother once said to me, "When one sees the tree in leaf one thinks the beauty of the tree is in its leaves, and then one sees the bare tree."

SAMUEL MENASHE
quoting Sarah Brana Barak

When Rabbi Bunam was lying on his deathbed, he said to his wife who wept bitterly: "Why do you weep? All my life has been given to me merely that I might learn to die."

Chasidic

In a dream we live seventy years and discover, on awakening, that it was a quarter of an hour. In our life which passes as a dream, we live seventy years, and then we waken to a greater understanding which shows us that it was a quarter of an hour. Perfect understanding is beyond time.

Chasidic

One wears his mind out in study, and yet has more mind with which to study. One gives away his heart in love, and yet has more heart to give away. One perishes out of pity for a suffering world, and is the stronger therefor. So, too, it is possible at one and the same time to hold on to life and let it go. . . .

MILTON STEINBERG

When we are dead, and people weep for us and grieve, let it be because we touched their lives with beauty and simplicity. Let it not be said that life was good to us, but, rather, that we were good to life.

JACOB P. RUDIN

What do our rabbis teach us about death? We know nothing of what is beyond the grave, and surely, the rabbis were strict about those who wanted to know what no man is given to know. But they taught us to pray: Blessed art Thou, O Lord, who art a true friend to those who sleep in the dust. The rabbis taught us to pray: Blessed art Thou, O Lord, who quickenest the dead. We do not die into the grave, we die into the eternity of God.

IGNAZ MAYBAUM

The cemetery – the "House of Life"

On the doorposts of many Jewish cemeteries there is written in Hebrew "The House of Life". It is as disconcerting as the text from the Bible "the day of death is better than the day of birth".

(Ecclesiastes 7:1)

"To walk humbly with your God" – these words are written over the gate which leads out of the mysterious, miraculous light of the divine sanctuary in which no man can remain alive.
Where do the wings of the gate open?
Do you not know? INTO LIFE.

FRANZ ROSENZWEIG

The Army of the Dead

Here in the cemetery
With its white regiments,
Each man, each coward and hero,
Is revealed to be equally brave,
Equally a veteran of the only important war there is,
The only one from which there is no discharge
And no return.
Life is no enlistment –
There'd be nobody left if it were.
Who would enrol himself a volunteer
In a contest with one sure-fire, fatal outcome?
All drafted, we drag out the long campaign
With various degrees of distinction,
But posthumously we're all decorated
With praise and flowers.
Which is as it should be.

MILTON HINDUS

Mourning

What *is* it like to be left alone after a death? It entails tremendous and exhausting acts of will to get through each day.

It means there is nowhere for an affectionate nature to put its affections. It means there is no one to whom one can say, "Any messages?" when one comes in. It means the dirty teacup still in the sink where, in a hurry, you left it. It means rooms filled with silence. It means no longer saying "We".

It means walking conversationally on eggs, learning not to utter sentences like "The X's invited me over last week, I think they knew I was having a bad time, but anyway I met this charming couple there. . . ."

Only you never finish this sentence, since at the words "bad time" your listeners frequently dive for cover, change the subject, move about . . . because they think (often very unjustly) that you're going to start talking about your situation again.

There are other things. One's personal dimensions somehow alter to the world outside; most clearly seen, I suppose, in the by now well-publicized troubles of the widow. The sudden drop in status, the invitations to tea instead of dinner parties. Your best friends can become suspicious, their husbands . . . let's say unpredictable.

Widowers too suffer greatly from social loneliness – or rather, the more discriminating do. The less sensitive (so many lonely women) can have a field day.

Loneliness. I have come at last to the word, the thing, the condition; the greatest bane of contemporary life. And especially the kind that comes after the absolute finality of a death.

GERDA CHARLES

Accusation

Dead friends
accuse you
that you have survived them

You weep over them
and laugh already
with other friends

Your flowers
on their graves
do not reconcile them

You mourn their death
and write poems
to life.

ROSE AUSLÄNDER

As a mother comforts her child,
so will I myself comfort you.

Isaiah 66:13

The last judgement

The nearest I ever got to a Judgement was not in a place of worship but on an analyst's couch. You risk more there. Counselling and therapy require courage.

In the future world man will be asked, "What was your occupation?" If he reply, "I fed the hungry", then they reply, "This is the gate of the Lord; he who feeds the hungry, let him enter" (Psalm 118:20). So with giving drink to the thirsty, clothing the naked, with those who look after orphans, and with those, generally, who do deeds of loving kindness. All these are gates of the Lord, and those who do such deeds shall enter within them.

Midrash Psalms

What will the judgement be like? Only this! God will take you one by one to Him and tell you what your life was really about. Then you will understand the good you did and the bad, and this will be your heaven and your hell. But after true knowledge comes forgiveness.

Chasidic (recounted by Joseph Weiss)

In the world to come the Holy One, blessed be He, will bring the impulse to evil and slay it in the presence of the righteous and wicked. To the righteous it will appear like a high mountain, to the wicked like a single hair. Both will weep. The righteous will weep and exclaim, "How were we able to subdue such a lofty mountain as this?" The wicked will weep and exclaim, "How were we unable to subdue a single hair like this?"

Succah

Our eternal home

The day is fading, the sun has set. Our father in heaven, quieten the doubts that rise within us, and our inner confusion, so that peace may find its way into our hearts and there make its home – Your peace which comes as we forgive others, and You forgive us.

Soon we shall journey from this house of prayer to our homes. May this peace we have sought here through our prayers and fasting return home with us, so that our homes can stand firm in life's storms, sheltering all that is generous and good in us from all that is mean and false.

For yet another home You have prepared for us, when our time on earth has ended: an eternal home more sure than all the earthly homes that we have known. The stars will soon appear in the dusk. Be our guiding star as we journey into life everlasting. And as the gates of this world close, open again the Gates of Mercy for us, and we shall enter in.

High Holyday Machzor

Our Home with God

Our home is a narrow crumbling path
That we tread as we long have trod,
Ice and hail, valleys and precipice,
Till we come home at night to God.

We all of us carry heavy sacks,
Precious gems in some, in others a useless load.
But whatever we bear our backs are bent by the weight,
Till we come home at night to God.

Some hurry, some crawl, it makes no difference at all.
Your road is measured off, each yard, each rod,
Some go miles, some from the cradle but an inch or two,
Till the horizon ends and we are home with God.

My hours grow shorter, more brief my days.
I go about with other people's tread that I have borrowed.
Any moment the sky on my road may fall,
And I shall find myself at home with God.

JOSEPH ROLNIK

Eternity

For a thousand years in Your sight are like
a yesterday gone by.

Psalm 90:4

9 · THE RIDDLE

Riddle of life

As in all riddles there is humour, but it is blacker than we want to imagine – more like Joe Orton than seems proper.

The whole world is but a little wheel,
Spun around by time.
Happiness and sorrow, honour and
  wealth,
Merely roll along by its side.

One lives his entire life in poverty,
The other lives in great wealth.
In the twinkling of an eye it all turns
  about,
With the spinning of the little wheel.

Brother, don't boast when you're
  well off,
In failure, do not lose heart.
Joy is not too far removed from
  distress,
For both can be changed by the little
  wheel.

Look at everything around you,
And learn a lesson thereby.
Then you will realize that rich and
  poor,
Depend only on the turn of the
  wheel.

TRADITIONAL YIDDISH

The world asks an old question:
Tra-la tra-di-ri-di-rom?
So the answer is: tra-di-ri-di-ri-lom,
Oy-ai, tra-di-ri-di-rom!
And if one wants to, one may also
    say: tra-i-dim?
So again we remain with the old
    question:
Tra-la-tra-di-ri-di-lom.

YIDDISH RIDDLE SONG

There is no definite distinction between games and real life. Some games have become big business, while many businessmen seek success as a game. Many of the rewards and losses in both are only in the mind: prestige, illusions of power, titles, etc.

On one of the days of Hanukkah, Rabbi Nahum, the son of the rabbi of Rizhyn, entered the House of Study at a time when he was not expected, and found his disciples playing draughts, as was the custom on those days. When they saw the zaddik they were embarrassed and stopped playing. But he gave them a kindly nod and asked: "Do you know the rules of the game of draughts?" And when they did not reply for shyness he himself gave the answer: "I shall tell you the rules of the game of draughts. The first is that one must not make two moves at once. The second is that one may only move forward and not backward. And the third is that when one has reached the last row, one may move to where he likes."

MARTIN BUBER

Why me?

What was most tragic in this Jewish tragedy of the twentieth century was that those who suffered it knew that it was pointless and that they were guiltless. Their forefathers and ancestors of medieval times had at least known what they suffered for; for their belief, for their law. They had still possessed a talisman of the soul which today's generation had long since lost, the inviolable faith in their God. . . . Only now, since they were swept up like dirt in the streets and heaped together, the bankers from their Berlin palaces and sextons from the synagogues of orthodox congregations, the philosophy professors from Paris and Rumanian cabbies, the undertaker's helpers and Nobel prize winners, the concert singers and hired mourners, the authors and distillers, the haves and the have-nots, the great and the small, the devout and the emancipated, the usurers and the sages, the Zionists and the assimilated, the Ashkenazim and the Sephardim, the just and the unjust, besides which the confused horde who thought that they had long since eluded the curse, the baptized and semi-Jews – only now, for the first time in hundreds of years, the Jews were forced into a community of interest to which they had long ceased to be sensitive, the ever-recurring – since Egypt – community of expulsion. But why this fate for them and always for them alone? What was the reason, the sense, the aim of this senseless persecution? They were driven out of lands but without a land to go to. They were expelled but not told where they might be accepted. They were held blameful but denied means of expiation. And thus, with smarting eyes, they stared at each other on their flight: Why I? Why you? How do you and I who do not know each other, who speak different languages, whose thinking takes different forms and who have nothing in common, happen to be here together? Why any of us? And none could answer.

STEFAN ZWEIG

We should be grateful to people in the holocaust who, though they had no answers, did not come up with too easy tinsel ones. Honest questions and honest doubt are worthy options. "Why me? Why now?" are reasonable questions when you are seriously ill. It is not your fault there are no reasonable answers – only glimmers of a distant purpose. Stefan Zweig committed suicide – the horror was too much for him.

It's not fair!

Just because life isn't fair, it doesn't mean you shouldn't make the best of it. Whatever game God is up to, it does not seem to be cricket!

If it be impossible for a man to have what he desires, he must desire what he has. Let him not prefer continual gloom. . . .

If we represent to ourselves that no misfortune will befall us, it is as though we desired not to exist at all. Because misfortunes are a necessary condition of the passing of worldly things.

SOLOMON IBN GABIROL

Rabbi Elazar Hakappar used to say: Without your consent you were born, and without your consent you live, and without your consent you die, and without your consent you will have to give an account and a reckoning before the King above the kings of kings, the Holy One, blessed be He.

Sayings of the Fathers 4:29

This is it.
There is no way of getting all you want.
There is no particular reason why you lost out on some
    things.
The world is not necessarily just. Being good often does not
    pay off
and there is no compensation for misfortune.
You don't really control anything.
You can't make anyone love you.
No one is stronger or weaker than anyone else.
Everyone is, in his own way, vulnerable.
We have only ourselves and one another.
That may not seem much but it is all there is.
You are free to do what you like, you need only face the
    consequences.

SHELDON KOPP

The essential contradiction in the human condition is that man is subject to force, and craves for justice. He is subject to necessity, and craves for the good. It is not his body alone that is thus subject, but all his thoughts as well; and yet man's very being consists in straining towards the good. That is why we all believe that there is a unity between necessity and the good. Some believe that the thoughts of man concerning the good possess the highest degree of force here below; these are known as idealists. They are doubly mistaken, first in that these thoughts are without force, and secondly in that they do not lay hold of the good. These thoughts are influenced by force; so that this attitude is in the end a less energetic replica of the contrary attitude. Others believe that force is of itself directed towards the good; these are idolaters. This is the belief of all materialists who do not sink into the state of indifference. They are also doubly mistaken; first force is a stranger to and indifferent to the good, and secondly it is not always and everywhere the stronger. They alone can escape these errors who have recourse to the incomprehensible notion that there is a unity between necessity and the good, in other words, between reality and the good, outside this world. These last also believe that something of this unity communicates itself to those who direct towards it their attention and their desire – a notion still more incomprehensible, but verified experimentally. . . .

SIMONE WEIL

Life is tough

Ol' Man River

Dere's an old man called the Mississippi.
Dat's the old man that I wants to be.
What does he care if the world's got trouble?
What does he care if the land ain't free?

Ol' man river
That ol' man river
He must know somethin'
But don't say nothin'
He just keeps rollin'
he keeps on rollin' along.

He don't plant 'taters.
He don't plant cotton
And them that plants them is soon forgotten
But ol' man river he just keeps rollin' along.

You and me we sweat and strain
Body all achin' and racked with pain.
Tote that barge and lift that bail.
You get a little drink and you lands in jail.

I get weary and sick of tryin'
I'm tired of livin' and scared of dyin'
But ol' man river
He just keeps rollin' along.

OSCAR HAMMERSTEIN II

Oscar Hammerstein who wrote it was a Jew, and Paul Robeson who sang it was a black. Both traditions know the toughness of life, so the song's sentiment is honest and still moves us.

It is ordained

Rabbi Akiba used to say,
Everything is foreseen, yet free choice is granted.

Sayings of the Fathers 3:19

*Bashert

These words are dedicated to those who died

These words are dedicated to those who died
because they had no love and felt alone in the world
because they were afraid to be alone and tried to stick it out
because they could not ask
because they were shunned
because they were sick and their bodies could not resist the
    disease
because they played it safe
because they had no connections
because they had no faith
because they felt they did not belong and wanted to die

These words are dedicated to those who died
because they were loners and liked it
because they acquired friends and drew others to them
because they took risks
because they were stubborn and refused to give up
because they asked for too much

ba-shert (Yiddish): inevitable, (pre)destined

These words are dedicated to those who died
because a card was lost and a number was skipped
because a bed was denied
because a place was filled and no other place was left

These words are dedicated to those who died
because someone did not follow through
because someone was overworked and forgot
because someone left everything to God
because someone was late
because someone did not arrive at all
because someone told them to wait and they just couldn't any
   longer

These words are dedicated to those who died
because death is a punishment
because death is a reward

because death is the final rest
because death is eternal rage

These words are dedicated to those who died

These words are dedicated to those who survived

These words are dedicated to those who survived
because their second grade teacher gave them books
because they did not draw attention to themselves and got
   lost in the shuffle
because they knew someone who knew someone else who
   could help them and bumped into them on a corner on a
   Thursday afternoon
because they played it safe
because they were lucky

These words are dedicated to those who survived
because they knew how to cut corners
because they drew attention to themselves and always got
   picked
because they took risks
because they had no principles and were hard

These words are dedicated to those who survived
because they refused to give up and defied statistics
because they had faith and trusted in God
because they expected the worst and were always prepared
because they were angry
because they could ask
because they mooched off others and saved their strength
because they endured humiliation
because they turned the other cheek
because they looked the other way

These words are dedicated to those who survived
because life is a wilderness and they were savage
because life is an awakening and they were alert
because life is a flowering and they blossomed
because life is a struggle and they struggled
because life is a gift and they were free to accept it

These words are dedicated to those who survived

IRENA KLEPFISZ

Self-fulfilling hypotheses and pseudo-events

You can approach the world religiously by asking what is good and what is bad in it. But there is another way, equally relevant, by asking what is true in it, and what is fake and phoney. Religion is also a forcing ground of fraud and hypocrisy, because the higher you rise the farther you can fall.

The intriguing feature of the modern situation, however, comes precisely from the fact that the modern newsmakers are not God. The news they make happen, the events they create, are somehow not quite real. There remains a tantalizing difference between man-made and God-made events.

A pseudo-event, then, is a happening that possesses the following characteristics:

1. It is not spontaneous, but comes about because someone has planned, planted, or incited it. Typically, it is not a train wreck or an earthquake, but an interview.

2. It is planted primarily (not always exclusively) for the immediate purpose of being reported or reproduced. Therefore, its occurrence is arranged for the convenience of the reporting or reproducing media. Its success is measured by how widely it is reported. Time relations in it are commonly fictitious or factitious; the announcement is given out in advance "for future release" and written as if the event had occurred in the past. The question "Is it real?" is less important than "Is it newsworthy?"

3. Its relation to the underlying reality of the situation is ambiguous. Its interest arises largely from this very ambiguity. Concerning a pseudo-event the question "What does it mean?" has a new dimension. While the news interest in a train wreck is in *what* happened and in the real consequences, the interest in an interview is always, in a sense, in *whether* it really happened and in what might have been the motives. Did the statement really mean what it said? Without some of this ambiguity a pseudo-event cannot be very interesting.

4. Usually it is intended to be a self-fulfilling prophecy. The hotel's thirtieth-anniversary celebration, by saying that the hotel is a distinguished institution, actually makes it one. . . .

Here are some characteristics of pseudo-events which make them overshadow spontaneous events.

1. Pseudo-events are more dramatic. A television debate between candidates can be planned to be more suspenseful (for example, by reserving questions which are then popped suddenly) than a casual encounter or consecutive formal speeches planned by each separately.

2. Pseudo-events, being planned for dissemination, are easier to disseminate and to make vivid. Participants are selected for their newsworthy and dramatic interest.

3. Pseudo-events can be repeated at will, and thus their impression can be reinforced.

4. Pseudo-events cost money to create; hence somebody has an interest in disseminating, magnifying, advertising and extolling them as events worth watching or worth believing. They are therefore advertised in advance, and re-run, in order to get money's worth.

5. Pseudo-events, being planned for intelligibility, are more intelligible and hence more reassuring. Even if we cannot discuss intelligently the qualifications of the candidates or the compli-

cated issues, we can at least judge the effectiveness of a television performance. How comforting to have some political matter we can grasp!

6. Pseudo-events are more sociable, more conversable and more convenient to witness. Their occurrence is planned for our convenience. The Sunday newspaper appears when we have a lazy morning for it. Television programmes appear when we are ready with our glass of beer. In the office the next morning, Jack Paar's (or any other star performer's) regular late-night show at the usual hour will overshadow in conversation a casual event that suddenly came up and had to find its way into the news.

7. Knowledge of pseudo-events – and what has been reported, or what has been staged, and how – becomes the test of being "informed". News magazines provide us regularly with quiz questions concerning not what has happened but concerning "names in the news" – what has been reported in the news magazines. Pseudo-events begin to provide that "common discourse" which some of my old-fashioned friends have hoped to find in the Great Books.

8. Finally, pseudo-events spawn other pseudo-events in geometric progression. They dominate our consciousness simply because there are more of them, and ever more.

DANIEL J. BOORSTIN

False charity

Among Rabbi Mendel's hasidim was a man by the name of Rabbi Moshe, who was both well-to-do and fond of doing good deeds. And then the wheel of fortune turned – to use a popular phrase – and he lost all his money and fell into debt. He went to the zaddik and told him about his predicament. "Go to my brother-in-law, the Seraph of Strelisk," said Rabbi Mendel, "and pour your heart out to him." The man did so. When Rabbi Uri of Strelisk had heard his story he said: "I shall take the bath of immersion for you and the merit of this bath will accrue to your benefit." The man returned to his master and reported what had happened. "Go back to my brother-in-law," said the rabbi of Kosov, "and say to him: 'The bath of immersion will not serve to pay my creditors.'"

The man rode to Strelisk a second time and said what he had

been told to. "Very well, my son", the Seraph replied. "In that case I shall also dedicate to your welfare the merit of the phylacteries which I shall put on today." When the man repeated this in Kosov, Rabbi Mendel said: "Give my brother-in-law this message from me: 'The phylacteries can't get rid of tormentors, either.' "

The man did as he was bidden. The Seraph reflected. "Well," said he, "if that is the case, I shall do my utmost for you. I shall dedicate to you the merit of all the prayers I say today, and thus from this hour on the three merits will unite in giving you help." Rabbi Moshe returned to Kosov and gave his report.

"Go," said the zaddik, and he spoke as softly as always, only more slowly, and when he spoke slowly the effect on those who were listening was greater than if he had raised his voice, "go, speak to my brother-in-law in my name and say: 'All this will not settle a single debt.' "

When the Seraph received this message, he immediately put on his fur coat and set out for Kosov. The moment he arrived at his brother-in-law's he asked: "What do you want of me?" "What I want," said Rabbi Mendel, "is for both of us to travel around for a number of weeks, and collect money from our people. For it is written: 'Thou shalt uphold him.' " And that is what they did.

MARTIN BUBER

True charity

The real thing!

Anne P., 44 Allen Street, front tenement, second floor. Husband Louis P. came here three years ago and one year ago sent for wife and three children. From that time unfortunately his trade, that of shoemaker, became less remunerative. She helped by washing and like labour, but two months ago he deserted her, though she stoutly maintains he returned to Odessa to get his old work back. The youngest, Meyer P., age five years, fell from the table and injured his hip. He lay for seven months in the Orthopaedic Hospital, 42nd Street; he was discharged as incurable and supplied with a brace. . . . The mother is absolutely tied by her pregnant condition; the cripple is in pain and cries to be carried. They had no rooms of their own but paid $5 a month to Hannah

A., a decent tailoress, who allowed the family to sleep on her floor. . . . Sunday I saw them. Monday I filed application with Montefiore Home for Meyer's admission. . . . Tuesday I went to Hebrew Sheltering Guardian Society, saw superintendent, and obtained promise of place for the two well children by Thursday. . . . Thursday afternoon we washed and dressed the two children, I left them in the afternoon at the Asylum, leaving my address for the superintendent so that he might know their friend in case of need. They have absolutely no one in America but their mother.

LILLIAN WALD, case notes from her pioneer
social work among poor immigrants to America

Often a man makes his heart do a charitable act, but the impulse to evil within him says: "Why practise charity and reduce your possessions? Rather than give to strangers, give to your children." But the good impulse prompts him to do charity.

Exodus Rabbah

Said the Leover: "If someone comes to you for assistance and you say to him: 'God will help you', you become a disloyal servant of God. It is for you to understand that God has sent you to aid the needy, and not to refer him back to God."

Chasidic

One can always find warm hearts who in a glow of emotion would like to make the whole world happy, but who have never attempted the sober experiment of bringing a real blessing to a single human being. It is easy to revel enthusiastically in one's love of man, but it is more difficult to do good to someone solely because he is a human being. When we are approached by a human being demanding his right, we cannot replace definite ethical action by mere vague good will. How often has the mere love of one's neighbour been able to compromise and holds its peace!

LEO BAECK

There are eight degrees in the giving of charity, one higher than
the other:

He who gives grudgingly, reluctantly, or with regret.

He who gives less than he should, but gives graciously.

He who gives what he should, but only after he is asked.

He who gives before he is asked.

He who gives without knowing to whom he gives, although
the recipient knows the identity of the donor.

He who gives without making his identity known.

He who gives without knowing to whom he gives, and the
recipient not knowing from whom he receives.

He who helps a fellowman to support himself by a gift, or a
loan, or by finding employment for him, thus helping him to
become self-supporting.

MAIMONIDES

Trying to understand our nationalism

*Religion and nationalism when taken together make people drunk or mad
– especially when neither is of the best quality. First-rate religion is more
soul searching, so it is not hijacked as easily. Examples are everywhere in
the Middle East and nearer home in Northern Ireland.*

The Jewish people, the separated people, therefore the holy
people, is a God-made people. In our nobility and in our shabbi-
ness, in our cultural refinement and in our vulgarity, in our
endurance and in our weakness, in our glory and in the shame of
our de-humanization in Auschwitz – we are the people of God; a
people not merely of believers in God – that we are too – but a
people in whom everyone, Jew himself and gentile alike, meets
his father in heaven who "will swallow up death for ever. . . .
And the shame of His people will He take away from off all the
earth" (Isaiah 25:8). We did not choose to be Jews, God has
chosen us.

IGNAZ MAYBAUM

Every people is a question which God addresses to humanity; and every people, from its place, with its special talents and possibilities, must answer for its own sake and for the sake of humanity.

LEO BAECK

If a man dislike his wife, he should not pray that God give him another wife, but rather, if she annoys him or is displeasing in his eyes, he should pray that God turn her heart to love him and to find favour in his eyes – so that they should renew their love for one another. . . . If one has an enemy, he should pray to the Holy One, not to slay or punish his enemy, but rather to help them both bring about peace. . . . In times of war, the prayer should not be for victory of the one side over the other, but it should be for peace – that the Holy One, blessed be He, influence their hearts that they make peace.

Sefer Chasidim

10 · THE RELIGIOUS QUEST

Hunting for God

There is a saying that God is the place of the world but the world is not His place. It is worth sitting back and figuring out such a statement.

A man was going from village to village, everywhere asking the same question, "Where can I find God?" He journeyed from rabbi to rabbi, and nowhere was he satisfied with the answers he received, so quickly he would pack his bags, and hurry on to the next village. Some of the rabbis replied, "Pray, my son, and you shall find Him". But the man had tried to pray, and knew that he could not. And some replied, "Study, my child, and you shall find Him". But the more he read, the more confused he became, and the further he seemed from God. And some replied, "Forget your quest, my child, God is within you". But the man had tried to find God within himself, and failed.

One day, the man arrived wearily at a very small village set in the middle of a forest. He went up to a woman who was minding some chickens, and she asked whom could he be looking for in such a small place, but she did not seem surprised when he told her that he was looking for God. She showed him to the Rabbi's house.

When he went in, the Rabbi was studying. He waited a moment, but he was impatient to be off to the next village, if he could not be satisfied. Then he interrupted, "Rabbi – how do I find God?" The Rabbi paused, and the man wondered which of the many answers he had already received he would be told this time. But the Rabbi simply said, "You have come to the right place, my child, God is in this village. Why don't you stay a few days; you might meet Him."

The man was puzzled. He did not understand what the Rabbi could mean. But the answer was unusual, and so he stayed. For two or three days, he strode round and round, asking all the villagers where God was that morning, but they would only smile, and ask him to have a meal with them. Gradually, he got to know them, and even helped with some of the village work. Every now and then he would see the Rabbi by chance, and the Rabbi would ask him, "Have you met God yet, my son?" And the man would smile, and sometimes he understood and sometimes he did not understand. For months he stayed in the village, and then for years. He became part of the village and shared in all its life. He went with the men to the synagogue on Friday and prayed with the rest of them, and sometimes he knew why he prayed, and sometimes he didn't. And sometimes he really said prayers, and sometimes only words. And then he would return with one of the men for a Friday night meal, and when they talked about God, he was always assured that God was in the village, though he wasn't quite sure where or when He could be found. Gradually, too, he began to believe that God was in the village, though he wasn't quite sure where. He knew, however, that sometimes he had met Him.

One day, for the first time, the Rabbi came to him and said, "You have met God now, have you not?" And the man said, "Thank you, Rabbi, I think that I have. But I am not sure why I met Him, or how or when. And why is He in this village only?"

So the Rabbi replied, "God is not a person, my child, nor a thing. You cannot meet Him in that way. When you came to our village, you were so worried by your question that you could not recognize an answer when you heard it. Nor could you recognize God when you met Him, because you were not really looking for Him. Now that you have stopped persecuting God, you have found Him, and now you can return to your town if you wish."

So, the man went back to his town, and God went with him. And the man enjoyed studying and praying, and he knew that God was within himself and within other people. And other people knew it too, and sometimes they would ask him, "Where can we find God?" And the man would always answer, "You have come to the right spot. God is in this place".

JEFFREY NEWMAN

Searching for God

Lord, where shall I find You?
High and hidden is Your place.
And where shall I not find You?
The world is full of Your glory.

I have sought Your nearness,
With all my heart I called You
and going out to meet You
I found You coming to meet me.

JUDAH HALEVI

Where could I go from Your spirit,
  or where could I flee from Your presence?
If I climb to heaven, You are there,
  there too, if I lie in the depths.
If I fly on wings to the dawn
  and dwell at the sea's horizon,
even there Your hand would lead me,
  Your right hand would hold me.
If I ask darkness to cover me
  and light to be night around me,
that darkness would not be dark to You,
  but night as bright as day
  and darkness like the light.

Psalm 139:7–12

When all within is dark,
and former friends misprise;
From them I turn to You,
and find love in Your eyes.

When all within is dark,
and I my soul despise;
From me I turn to You,
And find love in Your eyes.

When all Your face is dark,
and Your just angers rise;

From You I turn to You,
And find love in Your eyes.

ISRAEL ABRAHAMS
based on Ibn Gabirol

Where I wander – You!
Where I ponder – You!
Only You, You again, always You!
You! You! You!
When I am gladdened – You!
When I am saddened – You!
Only You, You again, always You!
You! You! You!
Sky is You, earth is You!
You above! You below!
In every trend, at every end,
Only You, You again, always You!
You! You! You!

LEVI YITZCHAK
of Berditchev

Meeting God

Meeting God can be very simple. If it is not simple, and no voice speaks in our silence, and no hand reaches down to meet ours in trust, then we should ask ourselves these questions, for the mistake may be ours.

Perhaps God cannot be Himself to us, because we are not ourselves, our true selves, to Him. We have not prayed to Him as we are, but as we feel we ought to be, or as others want us to be, or as what we think He thinks we ought to be. This last is the most difficult to unravel because it hides a confusion or a blasphemy.

Perhaps God meets us and we do not recognize Him. He may speak to us in a chance remark we overhear, through a stray thought in our mind, or by a word from the prayerbook that resonates in us. Perhaps a side door is the only door we have left open to Him. The others we defended and barred, so He must steal into us as a thief in the night.

Perhaps we do not like what He says, but are frightened to say so, and so pretend we never met Him, and indeed could not meet

Him, for He is only an idea. The avoidance is natural because in the sight of God our success can seem failure, and our ambitions dust.

Perhaps we are satisfied with our lives and do not want to meet Him. So we chant our prayers and sing our hymns to prevent a few moments' silence, for He speaks in the silence.

Perhaps we have not allowed God to judge us because we have already judged Him, and anticipated His word. He may love us more than we know; He may know us better than we know ourselves; He may still surprise us.

Perhaps we are frightened where He may lead us. He may send us from our father's house; He may bring us to the wilderness; He may let us wander in it for forty years; He may ask us to find our security in what we cannot touch. Will He give us courage equal to our need if we pray?

Meeting God can be simple, but nothing can happen if we do not will it. If we seek the Lord He can be found; He will allow us to find Him if we seek Him with all our might.

LIONEL BLUE

Losing faith

In the course of a religious life you lose faith and refind it many times, but each time it must be sought out on a deeper level. In a similar way during the course of one marriage, a couple are divorced and remarried many times.

I've Lost

I think I have lost something on the way,
What it is I do not know.
Shall I turn back? It is so far off now.
Yet it is a pity to let it go.

I have lost something, but do not know what.
Is it anything of worth?
I shall let it lie – for the day is short,
And vast is the earth.

Already the shadows fall from the trees.
Long falls my shadow.
My heart is unquiet. It cries – turn back.
My loss torments me so.

So I stand still in the midst of the road,
Tormented, doubt-tossed.
I have lost something, but do not know what.
But I know that I've lost.

ABRAHAM REISEN

We know of some very religious people who came to doubt God when a great misfortune befell them, even though they themselves were to blame for it; but we have never yet seen anyone who lost his faith because an undeserved fortune fell to his lot.

ARTHUR SCHNITZLER

Places of worship

The house of God will never close to them that yearn,
nor will the wicks die out that in the branches turn;
and all the pathways to God's house will be converging,
in quest of nests the migrant pigeons will come surging,
and when at close of crimson nights and frenzied days,
you'll writhe in darkness and will struggle in a maze
of demon's toils, with ashes strewn upon your head,
and lead-shot blood, and quicksand for your feet to tread,
the silent house of God will stand in silent glade.
It will not chide, or blame, or scoff, will not upbraid.
The door will be wide open and the light will burn,
and none will beckon you and none repel with stern
rebuke. For upon the threshold Love will wait to bless
and heal your bleeding wound and soothe your sore
distress . . .

YEHOASH

The tenderness is true but it needs to be tempered by this joke from popular "alternative" Judaism. Together they add up to the reality.
    A Jew was shipwrecked on a desert island. Two years later a

search party found him. Eagerly he showed them all he had done in his solitude. "Is that the home you built?", they asked, pointing to a hut of leaves and boughs. "No," he said severely, "it is the synagogue I built to pray in." They were touched. "And what is that other hut?", asked the search party. "That," said the shipwrecked Jew disdainfully, "is the synagogue I wouldn't be seen dead in!"

Clergy

When you're angry at the Rabbi you won't say Amen!

YIDDISH PROVERB

A disciple reported that his father had appeared to him in a dream and counselled him to become a Zaddik.

Hearing this, Simchah Bunam remarked: "The next time your father comes to you, ask him to appear in a dream to others, and persuade them to become your followers."

Chasidic

Cutting the cackle

I hate, I despise your feasts, and I take no delight in your solemn assemblies. Even though you offer Me your burnt offerings and cereal offerings, I will not accept them, and the peace offerings of your fatted beasts I will not look upon. Take away from Me the noise of your songs; to the melody of your harps I will not listen. But let justice roll down like waters, and righteousness like an ever-flowing stream.

Amos 5:21–24

He has told you, O man, what is good; and what does the Lord require of you: act justly, love mercy and walk humbly with your God.

Micah 6:8

Rabbi Simlai taught: Six hundred and thirteen commandments were given to Moses.

Then David reduced them to eleven in Psalm 15, beginning:

"He who follows integrity, who does what is right and speaks the truth in his heart."

Micah reduced them to three (Micah 6:8):

"Act justly, love mercy and walk humbly with your God."

Then came Isaiah and reduced them to two (Isaiah 56:1):

"Keep justice and act with integrity."

Amos reduced them to one (Amos 5:4):

"Seek Me and live."

Habakkuk also contained them in one (Habakkuk 2:4):

"But the righteous shall live by his faith."

Akiba taught:

"The great principle of the Torah is expressed in the commandment: 'Love your neighbour as you love yourself; I am the Lord' " (Leviticus 19:18).

But Ben Azai taught a greater principle (Genesis 5:1):

"This is the book of the generations of man. When God created man, He made him in the likeness of God."

Makkot

Hide and seek

When you call Me and come and pray to Me, I will hear you. When you seek Me, you will find Me, if you search for Me with all your heart. I shall let you find Me, says the Lord.

Jeremiah 29:12–14

The grandchild of Rabbi Baruch was playing hide-and-seek with another boy. He hid himself and stayed in his hiding place for a long time, assuming that his friend would look for him. Finally he went out and saw that his friend was gone, apparently not having looked for him at all, and that his own hiding had been in vain. He ran into the study of his grandfather, crying and complaining about his friend. Upon hearing the story Rabbi Baruch broke into tears and said: "God too says: 'I hide, but there is no one to look for me'."

A. J. HESCHEL

God's address

"Where is the dwelling of God?"

This is the question with which the Rabbi of Kotzk surprised a number of learned men who happened to be visiting him.

They laughed at him: "What a thing to ask! Is not the whole world full of His glory?"

Then he answered his own question:

"God dwells wherever man lets Him in."

MARTIN BUBER

True and false Gods

You shall have no other god but Me . . . for I, the Lord your God, am a jealous God.

Exodus 20:3,5

First comes Totoche, the god of Stupidity, with his scarlet monkey's behind, the swollen head of a doctrinaire and a passionate love for abstractions; he has always been the Germans' pet, but today he prospers almost everywhere, always ready to oblige; he is now devoting himself more and more to pure research and technology, and can be seen frequently grinning over the shoulders of our scientists; with each nuclear explosion his grin grows wider and wider and his shadow looms larger over the earth; his favourite trick is to hide his stupidity under the guise of scientific genius, and to enlist support among our great men to ensure our own destruction.

Then there is Merzavka, the god of Absolute Truth and Total Righteousness, the lord of all true believers and bigots; whip in hand, a Cossack's fur cap over one eye, he stands knee-deep in a heap of corpses, the eldest of our lords and masters, since time immemorial the most respected and obeyed; since the dawn of history he has had us killed, tortured and oppressed in the name of Absolute Truth, Religious Truth, Political Truth, Moral Truth; always with a capital "T" raised high above our heads, like a scaffold. One half of the human race obsequiously licks his boots, and this causes him immense amusement, for well he knows that there is no such thing as absolute truth, the oldest trick to goad us into slavery or to drive us at each other's throats. . . .

Then there is Filoche, the god of Mediocrity, full of bilious scorn and rabid prejudice, of hatred and petulance, screaming at the top of his voice, "You dirty Jew! You nigger! Jap! Down with the Yanks! Kill the yellow rats! Wipe out capitalists! Imperialists! Communists!" – lover of holy wars, a Great Inquisitor, who is always there to pull the rope at a lynching, to command a firing squad, to keep the jails full; with his mangy coat, his hyena's head and his deadly breath, he is one of the most powerful of the gods and the most eagerly listened to; he is to be found in every political camp, from right to left, lurking behind every cause, behind every ideal, always present, rubbing his hands whenever a dream of human dignity is stamped into the mud.

And Trembloche, the god of Acceptance and Servility, of survival at all costs, shaking with abject fear, covered with goose flesh, running with the hare and hunting with the hounds; a skilled persuader, he knows how to worm his way into a tired heart, and his white reptilian snout always appears before you when it is so easy to give up, and to remain alive takes only a little cowardice.

There are other gods, less easy to unmask, shifty and shrouded in mystery; their cohorts are innumerable and innumerable are the traitors amongst us ready to serve them; my mother knew them all; often, when the going was very hard, she would press my cheek against hers and point them out to me one by one; I listened, holding my breath, to the warning murmur and its promise of final victory, and soon those evil giants who bestride the world became for me more real than the most familiar objects in my nursery, and their towering shadows remain looming over me to this very day; I have only to raise my eyes to see the glitter of their armour in the sky, and their lances aimed at me in every beam of light.

ROMAIN GARY

Teachers

You catch religion, like you catch measles, from people – as much from what they are as from what they say.

Rabban Gamliel used to say: Find yourself a teacher.

Sayings of the Fathers 1:16

Rabbi Elazar said in the name of Rabbi Hanina: Whoever relates a thing in the name of the one who said it brings redemption into the world.

Megillah 15a

When a great Zaddik was asked why he did not follow the example of his teacher in living as he did, he replied: "On the contrary, I do follow his example, for I leave him as he left his teacher."

GERSHOM SCHOLEM

A disciple of Menachem Mendel of Kotzk complained: "Look, Rebbe! God created the universe in six days – and it's ugly!" "Would you have done better?" snapped Reb Mendel. "Eh, I think so", stammered the forlorn disciple. "Yes?" shouted the Kotzker Rebbe. "Then what are you waiting for? Start working – right now!"

Chasidic

This is the way of the Torah! A piece of bread with salt you will eat, a ration of water you will drink, upon the ground you will lie, a life of hardship you will lead, and you will labour in the Torah. If you do this, "happy shall you be" – in this world. "And it shall be well with you" – in the world to come.

Sayings of the Fathers 6:4

Cavalcade

Serve him his supper when the singer comes to call.
Take off his weariness and hang it in the hall.
He cannot stay long and his needs are very small
   And you may never see his like again.
   So hang on, don't be afraid
   You can join the cavalcade.

It isn't nice to see the way the prophet eats.
He tends to dribble and he's far too fond of sweets.
But when it matters he's the one who never cheats
   And you may never see his like again. . . .

Don't scare the poet who is hiding underground.
Though bombs are falling only he can hear the sound.
If words can heal you, better let him stay around
     And you may never see his like again. . . .

The teacher's tenderness, as strong as it is clear,
Using his glasses you can see beyond your fear
And watch with wonder as he'll slowly disappear
     And you may never see his like again. . . .

The grey-haired mother who likes her whisky neat
Without intending she's adopted half the street
Though she has nothing she will always make ends meet
     And you may never see her like again. . . .

The clown is innocent, the clown is very nice
And just enough a clown to have to pay the price
He's strangely wise but always takes the wrong advice
     And you may never see his like again. . . .

The scholar sits upon his unexpected throne
Giving a hint of the infinity he's known
Protected by a little whimsy of his own
     And you may never see his like again. . . .

The dancer waltzing through the nightmares of the past
Working with parables and dreams that have to last
Knowing the dangers when the music plays too fast
     And you may never see his like again. . . .

The cast assembled, the overture begins
Parading angels in their badly-fitting skins.
Off-stage the invisible director slowly grins
     And you may never see his like again.
     So hang on, don't be afraid
     You can join the cavalcade.

                                        JONATHAN MAGONET

*These refer to real people both of us know. First-class religion is not easy
to find, and they all had it. The "grey-haired mother" is no longer alive.
She was Anneliese Debray, a German woman who adopted thirteen
children, and us as well, along with assorted Turks, Poles, Israelis and
Arabs – and battered wives – indeed, anybody who was displaced in body
or spirit.*

Saviours

It was poets like Heine, and misfits like Karl Kraus and Kafka, who saw what could and did come. They were the prophets and seers of the twentieth-century apocalypse, not the clergy, especially the senior sort. Perhaps you can't be a prophet and part of the establishment – though pietists can be and so can priests.

Some of my cronies in the cafeteria near the *Jewish Daily Forward* in New York call me a pessimist and a decadent, but there is always a background of faith behind resignation. . . .

The pessimism of the creative person is not decadence, but a mighty passion for the redemption of man. While the poet entertains he continues to search for eternal truths, for the essence of being. In his own fashion he tries to solve the riddle of time and change, to find an answer to suffering, to reveal love in the very abyss of cruelty and injustice. Strange as these words may sound, I often play with the idea that when all the social theories collapse and wars and revolutions leave humanity in utter gloom, the poet – whom Plato banned from his Republic – may rise up to save us all.

ISAAC BASHEVIS SINGER

Messiahs

Rabbi Joshua came upon the prophet Elijah as he was standing at the entrance of Rabbi Simeon ben Yohai's cave.

He asked him: "When is the Messiah coming?"

The other replied: "Go and ask him yourself."

"Where shall I find him?"

"Before the gates of Rome."

"By what sign shall I know him?"

"He is sitting among poor people covered with wounds. The others unbind all their wounds at once, and then bind them up again. But he unbinds one wound at a time, and binds it up again straightway. He tells himself: 'Perhaps I shall be needed – and I must not take time and be late!' "

So he went and found him and said: "Peace be with you, my master and teacher!"

He answered him: "Peace be with you, son of Levi!"

Then he asked him: "When are you coming, master?"
He answered him: "Today!"

Thereupon he returned to Elijah and said to him: "He has deceived me, he has indeed deceived me! He told me, 'Today I am coming!' and he has not come."

But the other said to him: "This is what he told you: '*Today* – if ye would but hearken to His voice.'' (Psalm 95:7)

Sanhedrin 98a

The wise men and the prophets did not long for the days of the Messiah to seize upon the world, nor to rule over other faiths, nor to be glorified by nations, nor to eat, drink and have a good time, but to be free for Torah and its wisdom, free from oppression and distraction so that they might be fit for the life of the world to come. When that time is here, no one will go hungry; there will be no war, no fanaticism and no conflict, for goodness will flow abundantly and all delights will be as plentiful as the countless specks of dust, and the whole world will be only concerned with the knowledge of the Lord. Then the people of Israel will be truly wise for they will know what is hidden from us and they will attain that knowledge of their creator that it is humanly possible to attain, as it is written in the prophets: "For the earth shall be full of the knowledge of the Lord as the waters cover the sea."

MAIMONIDES

The future is made of the same stuff as the present. We are well aware that the good which we possess at present, in the form of wealth, power, consideration, friends, the love of those we love, the well-being of those we love, and so on, is not sufficient; yet we believe that on the day when we get a little more we shall be satisfied. We believe this because we lie to ourselves. If we really reflect for a moment we know it is false. Or again, if we are suffering illness, poverty, or misfortune, we think we shall be satisfied on the day when it ceases. But there too, we know it is false; so soon as one has got used to not suffering one wants something else. In the second place, we can decide not to confuse the necessary with the good. There are a number of things which we believe to be necessary for our life. We are often wrong, because we should survive if we lost them. But even if we are right, even if they are things whose loss might kill us or at least

destroy our vital energy, that does not make them good; because
no one is satisfied for long with purely and simply living. One
always wants something more; one wants something to live for.
But it is only necessary to be honest with oneself to realize that
there is nothing in this world to live for. We have only to imagine
all our desires satisfied; after a time we should become discon-
tented. We should want something else and we should be
miserable through not knowing what to want.

SIMONE WEIL

Thirty-six righteous people

*There is a Jewish legend concerning the Thirty-Six Just People. Their
number is constant in every age. They practise their goodness so humbly,
that no one ever knows who they are or their names. But they recognize
each other, and because of them and their goodness, the world survives. If
this seems fanciful, we do not know who set down the Torah or the
Gospels. We can never know the saintliness and unselfishness that
existed in the concentration camps or the Warsaw Ghetto. It might have
dazzled us.*

O Lord, remember not only the men and women of goodwill but
also those of illwill. But do not remember the suffering they have
inflicted upon us; remember the fruits we brought thanks to this
suffering, our comradeship, our loyalty, our humility, the courage, the generosity, the greatness of heart which has grown out of
this; and when they come to judgement, let all the fruits that we
have borne be their forgiveness.

The prayer of an unknown woman, found on a piece of
wrapping paper in Ravensbrück concentration camp

There is a reality outside the world, that is to say, outside space
and time, outside man's mental universe, outside any sphere
whatsoever that is accessible to human faculties.

Corresponding to this reality, at the centre of the human heart,
is the longing for an absolute good, a longing which is always
there and is never appeased by any object in this world. . . .

Just as the reality of this world is the sole foundation of facts, so
that other reality is the sole foundation of good.

That reality is the unique source of all the good that can exist in this world: that is to say, all beauty, all truth, all justice, all legitimacy, all order, and all human behaviour that is mindful of obligations.

Those minds whose attention and love are turned towards that reality are the sole intermediary through which good can descend from there and come among men.

SIMONE WEIL

Cautions about religion

The Baal Shem Tov once refused to enter a certain synagogue because he said it was too full of prayer. Noting his followers' astonishment at his attitude, he explained that so many routine insincere prayers were uttered there that they could not rise to the heavenly throne and stayed on earth, cramming the synagogue full.

BAAL SHEM TOV

Most of the people who come to a psychiatric department have not strayed very obviously from the straight and narrow. They are more likely to turn aggression against themselves rather than against others and to accuse themselves of acts of omission or commission. They are not, on the whole, the people who have committed unlawful acts, but are more likely to be casualties of their own harsh judgement on themselves.

A severely depressed person so often is the person who cannot allow himself to express the rage they feel about some hurt which they experienced in the past. The hurt may be one done to them by another person or it may be experienced as having been done by the Almighty, but since they cannot let themselves feel angry with parents or God, they believe that they must themselves be bad and worthless. . . .

The religious person may say that the individual's self-hatred can be transformed through the love of God, but in my experience he cannot feel the love of God if he has not felt the love of man. . . .

This is a truth the therapist comes up against constantly. The child who has never experienced parental love, affection and acceptance cannot feel loving towards other people, or towards God. It is very difficult to enable such a child to receive love from anyone because either he does not trust it or he simply cannot feel it.

IRENE BLOOMFIELD

Questions about religion

So many years ago when everybody was so old and wise and I was so young and naïve, Rosh Hashanah was the beginning of festivals of mystery. We lived in a small town in the hot and sandy desert of South-West Persia, and the New Year would arrive when the air was still arid as sand, the soil parched with thirst, and the sky blistered with the fire of the sun.

The frantic and pedantic cleaning of the house, always supervised by my grandmother, heralded the imminence of the festival. In the week before Rosh Hashanah the house smelt of sugar and honey, almonds and pomegranates, saffron and sweet wine. Then finally I was washed and scrubbed and dressed in new clothes, ready for the meal!!! We lived with my extended family, but as well as aunts and uncles and grandparents, there were always other guests. There were young men away from home on business, soldiers who were posted to the barracks in our town, and of course University students.

At dusk we would all sit around the white tablecloth always spread out on the patio floor next to the lime tree and the rose bushes, which was my grandfather's favourite place. The night was strange and my Jewishness a mystery and the meal had magic. Of course we ate apple and honey, but we also ate lamb's lung so that our sins would be considered as light as the lung, and I would wonder what was a sin? We asked God to strike down our enemies as we ate green beans and marrow. Where were all those enemies who hated me so much and yet I could not see them? And if my uncles each had as many children as the seeds of pomegranates there would be no room for all the children to sleep and we would have to build new rooms!

In the morning we would go to our small and simple and rather impecunious synagogue. It was built like a Spanish courtyard and people sat on benches all around it. In the middle was a raised platform and underneath that was the mikveh. I was always amazed at how rich the Sefer Torahs looked against the bare and multicoloured background. Even the glitter of all the jewels of the rich women could not match them.

The Sefer Torahs were the most ornate, the most magnificent, the most magical things on earth. The Rabbi performed the service regardless of everyone and with the help of no one. Most young men sat looking bored, only performing a duty. My grandfather and his friends fell into snoozes, their prayer shawls covering their heads and shoulders. Women chatted and prayed vehemently for their families while suckling their babies. And children played hide and seek around the columns and ate fruit and bread.

But all the time I imagined that it was a fairy tale castle *made* to look ordinary so that those who could not understand the light and mystery of being Jewish would not come to destroy it. Somehow I believed if I could only apprehend that magical language of Torah, then suddenly this old and dirty place with its ordinary people would transform into a cool and magnificent Garden of Eden.

But all that was so many years ago and in a different country. Now I try very hard to reason the question of my being, my identity, my quest. And yet somehow those far off days with their almost irreligious mysteries and oriental paradox bring my heart far nearer to Him than all my readings and reasonings.

MARY NIKNAM

Pious fools

Who is a pious man who is a fool? He who sees a woman drowning and says: It is unseemly for me to look at her, therefore I cannot rescue her.

Sotah 21b

Who is the pious fool? He who sees a child struggling in the water and says: When I have taken off my phylacteries I will go and save him, and while he does so the child dies.

Yerushalmi Sotah 3:4

The Pious Men of –

Oh God, help me!
For I have fallen into the hands of the righteous
And the sons of the pious have encompassed me.
Their gentle hands are choking my life from me,
Their pinky lips glow black with my blood.

Oh God, help me!
Have I not sacrificed to You my youth and strength?
Have I not searched for You along this road?
Have I not prayed unto You morning, noon and eve?
And now the lips of the pious dribble black with my blood.

Oh God, help me!
Help me and I shall give to You a noble gift;
For I will bind the pious and the righteous,
And I shall slay their God-enfeebling thoughts
And raise their cleans-ed souls a gift to Thee!

IZAK GOLLER

Checklist

Before his death, Rabbi Zusya said: "In the coming world, they will not ask me: 'Why were you not Moses?' They will ask me: 'Why were you not Zusya?'"

Chasidic

> If I am not for myself, who is for me?
> But if I am only for myself, what am I?
> And if not now, when?

HILLEL

How shall I come into the presence of the Lord, and bend low before God on high?

Micah 6:6

What are we?
What is our life?
What is our love?
What is our justice?
What is our success?
What is our endurance?
What is our power?
Lord our God, and God of our ancestors,
what can we say before You?

Siddur

Arguing with God

Jewish literature is helpful because it is more concerned with argument than decision, and debate than dogma. It is easily used by people trying to find their own way to faith. We were after all created free-range, not pious battery birds. It is not God who denies us freedom, it is we who can't take it, in every sense.

The Lord said: "Shall I hide from Abraham what I am about to do, seeing that Abraham shall become a great and mighty nation and all the nations of the earth shall be blessed through him? I have chosen him so that he may command his children and household after him to keep the way of the Lord by doing righteousness and justice so that the Lord may bring upon Abraham all that He has promised him." So the Lord said: "Because the cry of Sodom and Gomorrah is great and their sin is very grave, I will go down to see. If they have done according to the outcry that has come up to me, then destruction! But if not, then I will know."

The men had turned from there and gone to Sodom, but Abraham was still standing before the Lord. Then Abraham drew near and said: "Will you also wipe out the righteous together with the wicked? Suppose there are fifty righteous people in the city, will you wipe it out and not spare the place for the sake of the fifty righteous people within it? It would be a profanation to You to do such a thing, to bring death to the righteous together with the wicked! It would be a profanation to You! Shall the judge of all the earth not do justice?"

Genesis 18:17–25

In every era the attempt must be made to wrest tradition away from a conformism that is about to overpower it.

WALTER BENJAMIN

The traditional highway to God in Judaism is argument – but you have to trust to use it and not many are that secure. It is easier to suppress and be rude to those opponents who give voice to your own doubts.

When the great Rabbi Israel Baal Shem Tov saw misfortune threatening the Jews it was his custom to go into a certain part of the forest to meditate. There he would light a fire, say a special prayer, and the miracle would be accomplished and the misfortune averted.

Later, when his disciple, the celebrated Magid of Mezritch, had occasion, for the same reason, to intercede with heaven, he would go to the same place in the forest and say: "Master of the Universe, listen! I do not know how to light the fire, but I am still able to say the prayer", and again the miracle would be accomplished.

Still later, Rabbi Moshe Leib of Sasov, in order to save his people once more, would go into the forest and say: "I do not know how to light the fire, I do not know the prayer, but I know the place and this must be sufficient." It was sufficient and the miracle was accomplished.

Then it fell to Rabbi Israel of Rizhyn to overcome misfortune. Sitting in his armchair, his head in his hands, he spoke to God: "I am unable to light the fire and I do not know the prayer, I cannot even find the place in the forest. All I can do is tell the story, and this must be sufficient." And it was sufficient.

ELIE WIESEL

Arguing with ourselves

I could say that I am suffering from a split consciousness. There are two forces inside of me, each seeking to dominate the other. One I experience as a masculine, assertive force. I am manipulative and egocentric, and I have an urge to be dominating and authoritarian. My intellect enjoys having answers, possessing truths. Mind, will and logic dominate. That part of me is pulled to *halakhah* (law) and order, argument and debate, looking for a fixed and secure Jewish framework in which to orientate my daily life. This force in me endlessly seeks an anthology of traditional practice in which I can anchor myself against the rootlessness and the superficial truths which pervade my Western life. When it is over-emphasized, however, I experience it as destructive. It is ambitious and greedy: it enjoys judging, owning, using. It has to be right. It wants its own way. It is often detached and aloof.

The other force is not concerned with having and using. It is concerned with feelings and sensitivity, dreams, creativity, fantasy, *aggadah* (lore). It is intuitive, gentle and strong. It allows me to be receptive, allowing and accepting. When I live from this still centre I do not need to manipulate people and events to suit my own needs. I experience this force as a powerful feminine one, in which my ego submits to a power greater than myself. Its concern is my growth, development and change as a human being. It is the force of *rachamim*, which, as the Biblical root *rechem* (womb) suggests, is the creative force acting as a gestation process, and working towards my gradual emergence as a being living in harmony with God's will rather than my own. I have come to identify that place of inner calm as my own soul, where God dwells: "Just as the Holy One, blessed be He, is pure, so is the soul pure." The times when I am able to live from that centre enable me to see myself, others and the situations in which I find myself more clearly. This force is concerned with honesty rather than self-deception, real truth rather than what I would like to be true.

HOWARD COOPER

To yourself be true

The Holy Cow

I love listening to Indian devotional songs. They seem pure, like water drawn from a well; and the emotions they express are both beautiful and easy to understand because the imagery employed is so human. The soul crying out for God is always shown as the beloved yearning for the lover in an easily recognizable way ("I wait for Him. Do you hear His step? He has come"). I feel soothed when I hear such songs and all my discontentment falls away. I see that everything I have been fretting about is of no importance at all because all that matters is this promise of eternal bliss in the Lover's arms. I become patient and good and feel that everything is good. Unfortunately this tranquil state does not last for long, and after a time it again seems to me that nothing is good and neither am I. Once somebody said to me: "Just see, how sweet is the Indian soul that can see God in a cow!" But when I try to assume this sweetness, it turns sour: for, however much I may try and fool myself, whatever veils I may try, for the sake of peace of mind, to draw over my eyes, it is soon enough clear to me that the cow *is* a cow, and a very scrawny, underfed, diseased one at that. And then I feel that I want to keep this knowledge, however painful it is, and not exchange it for some other that may be true for an Indian but can never quite become that for me.

And here, it seems to me, I come to the heart of my problem. To live in India and be at peace one must to a very considerable extent become Indian and adopt Indian attitudes, habits, beliefs, assume if possible an Indian personality. But how is this possible? And even if it were possible – without cheating oneself – would it be desirable? Should one want to try to become something other than what one is? I don't always say no to this question. Sometimes it seems to me how pleasant it would be to say yes and give in and wear a sari and be meek and accepting and see God in a cow. Other times it seems worth while to be defiant and European and – all right, be crushed by one's environment, but all the same have made some attempt to remain standing. Of course, this can't go on indefinitely and in the end I'm bound to lose – if only at the point where my ashes are immersed in the Ganges to the accompaniment of Vedic hymns, and then who will say that I have not truly merged with India?

I do sometimes go back to Europe. But after a time I get bored there and want to come back here. I also find it hard now to stand the European climate. I have got used to intense heat and seem to need it.

RUTH PRAWER JHABVALA

The importance of atheists

Rabbi Moshe Leib said:

"There is no quality and there is no power of man that was created to no purpose. And even base and corrupt qualities can be uplifted to serve God. When, for example, haughty self-assurance is uplifted it changes into a high assurance in the ways of God. But to what end can the denial of God have been created? This too can be uplifted through deeds of charity. For if someone comes to you and asks your help, you shall not turn him off with pious words, saying: 'Have faith and take your troubles to God!' You shall act as if there were no God, as if there were only one person in all the world who could help this man – only yourself."

MARTIN BUBER

A European in the latest mode of dress,
An atheist, an advanced, progressive man,
Yet I have suddenly stopped in my stride,
And fling my arms out – Save and bless!

My suit hangs badly on me, doesn't fit.
My tie is like a rope around my neck,
When the lightning flashes high in heaven,
And the thunder crashes all over it.

I am afraid, therefore I come to You,
Not fawning, not begging, but in despair
I beat both my fists upon Your door,
That You may comfort me and reassure.

I need You, like a mother and a home.
I need You like the bread that comes to me like blood,
Because I am alone,
And don't know what's the good.

MOSHE SHIMMEL

Returning

A king had a son who had gone astray from his father a journey of a hundred days. His friends said to him: "Return to your father." He said: "I cannot." Then his father sent to say: "Return as far as you can, and I will come to you the rest of the way." So God says, "Return to Me, and I will return to you."

Pesikta Rabbati

The gates of repentance are always open.

Pesikta d'Rav Kahana

There is no doubt that it is very easy for a believer to forget his belief completely and to live, even for years, untouched by the memory of God; either because he is too happy or too absorbed in his happiness to find any use in God, or else because he is so lost in suffering that he does not seem able to give God insults or tears, and prefers silence. Talking to God would mean talking to himself as well, and he no longer talks to himself. He feels that he has somehow turned to stone, and sometimes he remembers confusedly that God has no truck with stone. . . .

There are times in which he feels he is turning to God in great anger, and these are the only times when he feels words foaming up in him with which he can speak to God. He wants to blame God, as he wants to slap a human being in the face; a human being whose behaviour seems senseless, inexplicable and absurd, full of irrevocable mistakes. He and his life seem surrounded by wrongs and misfortunes, and he sees himself and all the people he knows thrashing about in hopeless situations. . . .

And yet if he thinks back to these moments, he feels not at all sure that God disliked them in him. Other moments God must have disliked far more; when, for instance, through cowardice, he stooped to actions that were soft or ignoble, when he was ungrateful to someone who had given him a great deal, or toyed with ideas that were vain and cynical, when he was indifferent or distracted with someone who asked him for help, or promised to help someone and then did nothing about it. . . .

When he looks back on this outburst of rage, he suddenly finds it comic; and as he does so, and laughs at himself, he feels, as he always feels when he laughs heartily at himself, deep in his own spirit, trembling and fluttering, something that vanishes in a moment and which, perhaps, is God.

NATALIA GINSBURG

Religion and magic

God must also be thought capable of saying "No!" Perhaps this is indeed the major difference between engaging in magic and engaging in prayer. Magic, by definition, *must* work. If it does not yield results, then, in the view of the practitioner of magic, something must have gone wrong with the performance of the magical rite; and he will repeat the rite in a more careful and meticulous manner. Prayer, on the other hand, is addressed to a God who has a will and a mind of His own. God cannot be manipulated by man. He can only be *addressed*. He may, or may not grant a specific request. But there is no mechanism of man's devising which would compel Him to do so. In addressing God, man knows that a "No" can be as much of an "answer" as a "Yes".

JAKOB J. PETUCHOWSKI

Religious suffering is at one and the same time the expression of real suffering and a protest against real suffering. Religion is the sigh of the oppressed creature, the heart of a heartless world and the soul of soulless conditions. It is the opium of the people.

KARL MARX

It is tragically true that we are often wrong about God, believing in that which is not God, in a counterfeit ideal, in a dream, in a cosmic force, in our own father, in our own selves. We must never cease to question our own faith and ask what God means to us. Is He an alibi for ignorance? The white flag of surrender to the unknown? Is He a pretext for comfort and unwarranted cheer? A device to cheat despondency, fear or despair?

From whom should we seek support for our faith if even religion can be a fraud, if by self-sacrifice we may hallow murder? From our minds which have so often betrayed us? From our conscience which easily fumbles and fails? From the heart? From our good intentions? "He that trusts in his own heart is a fool" (Proverbs 28:26). "The heart is deceitful above all things, it is exceedingly weak – who can know it?" (Jeremiah 17:9).

A. J. HESCHEL

Resignation

They're writing songs of love,
  But not for me;
A lucky star's above,
  But not for me.

With Love to Lead the Way,
I've found more Clouds of Grey
Than any Russian play
  Could guarantee.

I was a fool to fall
  And Get That Way;
Heigh ho! Alas! and al-
  So, Lackaday!

Although I can't dismiss
The mem'ry of his kiss –
  I guess he's not for me.

IRA GERSHWIN

I took myself back to New York to think that trouble makes trouble, and that is what is most to be feared about it. I was learning that change, loss, an altered life, is only a danger when you become devoted to disaster.

Money was beginning to go and go fast. I had gone from earning a hundred and forty thousand a year (before the movie blacklist) to fifty and then twenty and then ten, almost all of which was taken from me by the Internal Revenue Department, which had come forward with its claim on the sale of a play that the previous administration had seemingly agreed to. I didn't understand it then and I don't now; my lawyer advised a compromise. But the compromise allowed was small, and the collection very large.

The loss of money made less difference than I thought; middle-class security is a faith from which I have never recovered, but that has certain virtues.

LILLIAN HELLMAN

Nothing comes to man except by the decree of the Holy One, blessed be He. One should pray for God's mercy that whatever is decreed shall turn out for the sake of heaven.

Sefer Chasidim

> Within His hand I lay my soul
> both when I sleep and when I wake,
> and with my soul my body too. . . .
>
> *Siddur*

Without the mystery what's left?

The most beautiful and deepest experience a man can have is the sense of the mysterious. . . . He who never had this experience seems to me, if not dead, then at least blind. To sense that behind anything that can be experienced there is a something that our mind cannot grasp and whose beauty and sublimity reaches us only indirectly and as a feeble reflection, *this* is religiousness. In *this* sense I am religious.

ALBERT EINSTEIN

The world is full of meaning precisely because in its totality it remains veiled, incomprehensible, a revealed and hidden secret which, if we gain even the slightest awareness of its existence, fills us with awe and amazement, with an unendurable shudder. . . . Without these . . . the world is nothing more than an oversized slaughterhouse.

HILLEL ZEITLIN

Seeing stars

> When I look up at Your heavens, the work of Your hands,
> the moon and the stars You set in place,
> what is man that You should remember him,
> or the son of man that You should care for him.
>
> Psalm 8:4–5

God was always the beginning and the end of all my thoughts. If now I ask: What is God? what His nature? even as a small child I already asked: What is God like? what does He look like? And at that time I could spend whole days looking up at the sky, and in the evening I was quite disconsolate, that I had never glimpsed the most holy countenance of God, but had only seen the silly grimaces of the grey clouds. I grew entirely confused by all the information learned from astronomy, which subject even the smallest child was not spared in that period of enlightenment. I could not get over the wonder of it, that all these thousands of millions of stars were great and beautiful globes, like our own, and that one simple God ruled over all these gleaming myriads of worlds. Once in a dream, I remember, I saw God, in the farthest distance of the high heavens. He was gazing contentedly out of a little window of heaven, a pious old face with a little Jewish beard; He was scattering handfuls of seeds, which as they fell from heaven opened out, as it were, in the immeasurable space, and grew to tremendous size, until they finally became bright, flourishing, inhabited worlds, each one as large as our own. I have never been able to forget this face; I often saw this cheerful old man in my dreams again, scattering the seeds of worlds out of His tiny window: I once even saw Him cluck with his lips, just as our maid used to do when she gave the hens their barley. I could only see the falling seeds, always expanding to vast shining globes: but the great hens, which were possibly lying in wait somewhere with wide-open beaks, to be fed with these world-spheres, those I could never see.

HEINRICH HEINE

There are stars whose light reaches the earth only after they
    themselves have disintegrated and are no more.
And there are men whose shining memory lights the world after
    they have passed from it.
These lights which shine in the darkest night are those which
    illumine for us the path.

HANNAH SENESH

God full of compassion whose presence is over us, grant perfect rest beneath the shelter of Your presence with the holy and pure on high who shine as the lights of heaven, to . . . . who has gone to her everlasting home. Master of mercy, cover her in the shelter of Your wings for ever, and bind her soul into the

gathering of life. It is the Lord who is her heritage. May she be at
peace in her place of rest. Amen.

MEMORIAL PRAYER

I find it is Yom Kippur,
                    and here I am
Down by the river
                    in late afternoon.
There is a poem
                    I have read
In several versions,
                    about the Jewish writer
Who doesn't fast, who
                    doesn't go to synagogue
On Yom Kippur,
                    the day of atonement,
And here is my construction
                    of that poem.
Here am I,
            on the embankment
Staring at the river,
                    while the lights
Are coming up,
            signifying darkness, the end of the fast,
Though it's not over yet,
                    and the congregations
Are still gathered
                    in the synagogues,
Praying, *slach lonu, m'chal lonu,*
                    forgive us, pardon us,
We have sinned,
                    we deserve punishment,
We are like clay
                    in the hands of the great Potter,
Who has shaped us all,
                    even, you could say, me
Here by the river,
                    watching the water
And the rubbish
                    drifting on the water,

Imagining what is
                    swaying in under the bridges,
Is something of exile,
                    formless but perceptible,
Bringing in the names
                    of pious cities,
Vilna and Minsk and Vitebsk
                    (my own ancestral names)
And vanished communities,
                    behind curtains
Of forgetfulness,
                    and ordinary human change,
Praying communities
                    on Yom Kippur and other days
Clinging to and turning from
                    that which I cling to
And turn from,
                    if you like the covenant
That keeps me fasting,
                    but not in synagogue
Today, Yom Kippur.
                    I go into the gardens
Sit down on a bench,
                    read my newspaper,
And wait
          for the first star.

                                        ARTHUR JACOBS

Jews still use a modified version of the lunar calendar they inherited from the Babylonians. Therefore the new day begins at dusk when the first stars appear in the sky, not at night or sunrise.

The feeling of the Day of Atonement (Yom Kippur) and its seriousness and concern with sin have their counterpart in Christian Lent.

Everything may change in our demoralized world except the heart, man's love and his striving to know the Divine. Painting, like all poetry, has a part in the Divine; people feel this today just as much as they used to. What poverty surrounded my youth, what trials my father had with us nine children. And yet he was always full of love and in his way a poet. Through him I first sensed the existence of poetry on this earth. After that I felt it in the nights, when I looked into the dark sky. Then I learnt that there was also another world. This brought tears to my eyes, so deeply did it move me.

MARC CHAGALL

11 · ALL HAVING BEEN SAID

Graffiti

Inscription on the walls of a cellar in Cologne, Germany, where Jews hid from the Nazis:

> I believe in the sun when it is not shining.
> I believe in love even when feeling it not.
> I believe in God even when He is silent.

Wise sayings we don't understand

A bed is always comfortable if you make it that way.

GERTRUDE STEIN

Everyone sits in the prison of his own ideas.

ALBERT EINSTEIN

A man is like a carpenter. A carpenter lives and lives and then he dies. And the same with a man.

SCHALOM ALEICHEM

Comparing One to Another

Someone once told Rabbi Mendel that a certain person was greater than another whom he also mentioned by name. Rabbi Mendel replied: "If I am I because I am I, and you are you because you are you, then I am I, and you are you. But if I am I because you are you, and you are you because I am I, then I am not I, and you are not you."

MARTIN BUBER

EPILOGUE

Lionel offered me the last word, which is always a risk in this sort of partnership. We have been doing a religious double-act together through twenty years of youth movements, prayer-books, conferences, committees and interfaith dialogues – but we found the resources to keep us going in special friends and teachers and in conversations in railway stations, assorted cafés and bars throughout Europe, or while walking Lionel's various dogs round London's open spaces. The visible part of this book is newly assembled, the invisible part took, as they say, the best part of a lifetime.

It has been a strange journey, separately and together, along the margins of Jewish religious life, in that no-man's-land where the reality of people's experience rubs uncomfortably against the conventions of institutionalized religion. Along the way we even found our respective niches in a small corner of the Jewish "establishment", but we both need to keep one foot in outside realities. That is probably what gives this collection any value it may have – our fascination with exploring Jewish wisdom through unconventional routes and unexpected sources, but also with letting the tradition loose, with all its stunning richness, quirkiness and challenge, on the wider world.

I fell in love with the Hebrew Bible as a Rabbinic student when I learnt how subversive it could be, how consistently it works against the conventions of its time and of ours. Later Jewish teachings can have the same effect though they are much less accessible. For all their engagement with the details of life, they have a certain detachment, a divine amusement or sadness at our human self-importance. At times of success the Torah has pre-vented Jewish pride from overwhelming us and, in tragic periods, Jewish suffering from diminishing us.

Anthologies like this have to stand by themselves – but what if you want to read on? Then you have at least two choices – there are always two choices (see page 52).

There are now a lot of other anthologies, popular histories of, and introductions to, Judaism. Try some Jewish interpretations of the Hebrew Bible. They are often quite startling and refreshing if you only know Christian or "biblical scholarship" ways of reading the "Old Testament". Collections like Ginzberg's *Legends of the Jews*, the Montefiore and Loewe *A Rabbinic Anthology*, and Buber's *Tales of the Hasidim* are classics and easily accessible. So one choice is to take some more "lucky dips" into Jewish thought and tradition.

The other choice is harder. The great sources of Jewish teaching, like the Talmud and Midrash, need years of disciplined study – and the acquiring of a couple of languages (Hebrew and Aramaic). But don't be put off. A friend of mine, a seventy-year-old nun, attended a Jewish-Christian Bible Week in Germany some years ago and learnt the Hebrew alphabet. She was back a year later armed with an advanced Hebrew grammar, and from then on consulted her own Hebrew Bible. Abraham did not start his journey till he was seventy, and if he had given up we would none of us be here.

There is, of course, a middle way – which is to take the advice of the Rabbis and "find yourself a teacher and get yourself a friend" (*Sayings of the Fathers 1:16*), and dip your toe in together. There are probably classes at your local synagogue, though they may be a bit surprised at your interest, if you're Christian, and astonished if you're Jewish – sadly, we are not an educated Jewish generation.

But Judaism does not really exist in a vacuum or on the pages of a book. It is the lived experience, pain, struggle and joy, of a people on a bewildering, and not always welcome, journey through history. Jews today feel particularly vulnerable because of the recent past, but Judaism has rarely been so readily accessible to seekers of old and new truths. If this little collection of "travellers' tales" can show you a glimpse of the journey then it will have more than served its purpose. "Blessed is the one who comes in the name of the Lord."

JONATHAN MAGONET

Who's Who

ABRAHAMS, ISRAEL (1858–1924) British scholar and lecturer in Hebrew and Jewish studies. Founder member of Liberal Judaism in Britain. His many works include *Jewish Life in the Middle Ages*.

ADLER, ALFRED (1870–1937) Austrian psychiatrist, later settled in America. Part of the circle around Sigmund Freud, he left it to develop his theory of Individual Psychology.

AKIBA BEN JOSEPH (*c.* 50–*c.* 135 CE) Most prominent among early Rabbinic teachers. Began to study late in life, introduced systematization of law and developed new methods for interpreting Bible. Supported Bar Kochba's rebellion and died as a martyr.

ALLAN, ELIZABETH Contemporary. Born in Bombay, settled in Britain.

ARENDT, HANNAH (1906–75) Political and social philosopher. Born Germany, settled in the United States in 1941. Works include *Eichmann in Jerusalem: A Report on the Banality of Evil* and *The Origins of Totalitarianism*.

ASCH, SHOLEM (1881–1957) Yiddish novelist and dramatist, born in Poland. Wrote about Eastern Europe and Biblical subjects, also Christian themes.

AUSLÄNDER, ROSE b. 1918 Bukovina. Poet living in Germany.

BAAL SHEM TOV (The Besht) "Master of the Good Name". (Israel ben Eliezer. *c.* 1700–60). Founder of Chasidism. Stressed the joyful observance of commandments and popularized Kabbalistic teachings.

BAECK, LEO (1873–1956) Rabbi, teacher of Midrash and Homiletics in Berlin (*Hochschule für die Wissenschaft des Judentums*). Elected head of the representative council of the Jews in Germany in 1933, and stayed with his congregation until he was sent to Theresienstadt in 1943. Survived the war and settled in London. Books include *The Essence of Judaism* and *This People Israel*.

BARAK, SARAH BRANA – See MENASHE.

BEGIN, MENACHEM b. 1913 in Brest Litovsk, settled in Palestine in 1942. A Zionist activist he was imprisoned by Polish and later Russian authorities, having escaped from the Nazis. In Palestine he led an underground struggle against the British Mandate. As Prime Minister of Israel he signed the peace agreement with President Sadat of Egypt.

BELLOW, SAUL b. 1915. American

novelist whose characters, many of them Jewish, search for ultimate reality in the modern world. Nobel Prize for Literature.

BENJAMIN, WALTER (1892–1940) German Marxist philosopher, literary critic and translator. Under threat of being sent back to Nazi-occupied France from the Spanish border he took his life. His essays are in several collections including *Illuminations*.

BERDITCHEV, LEVI YITZHAK OF (THE BERDITCHEVER) (1740–1809) Chasidic leader, pupil of Dov Baer of Mezritch. Central doctrine was "love for Israel".

BERENSON, BERNARD (1865–1959) American art historian and connoisseur. A prolific writer, he helped establish the identity of Renaissance artists. He bequeathed to Harvard University his villa near Florence which housed art treasures and a library.

BERGMAN, ALEXANDER (1912–41) American poet. Bedridden for three years before his death, his poems on hospital life, love and death were published in *They Look Like Men*.

BERLE, MILTON (Berlinger) b. 1908. American comedian, film and television performer.

BERLIN, IRVING (Baline) b. 1888 in Russia. American composer and songwriter. With over 1000 compositions, one of the shapers of the popular American song. He wrote for the stage and films and his successes included *White Christmas*.

BESHT – see BAAL SHEM TOV.

BETTELHEIM, BRUNO b. 1903. Psychologist and educationalist; pioneered treatment of emotionally disturbed children. Born in Vienna, settled in the United States in 1939. Controversial critic of Jewish responses to Nazi terror. Author of *The Informed Heart* and *Dynamics of Prejudice*.

BLOOMFIELD, IRENE b. 1918. Psychotherapist, director of the Raphael Centre, a Jewish counselling service. Born Germany, emigrated to England 1937. Teaches counselling at the Leo Baeck College.

BLUE, LIONEL b. 1930. British Reform Rabbi, Convener of the Reform Beth Din. Co-editor of the Daily and Sabbath Prayer Book, and the High Holy Day Prayer Book. Broadcaster and religious writer. Author of *To Heaven with Scribes and Pharisees*.

BOERNE, LUDWIG (1786–1837) German political essayist and champion of Jewish emancipation. Criticized by Heine.

BOMZE, NACHUM (1906–54) Yiddish poet. Served with the Red Army. Emigrated to USA.

BOORSTIN, DANIEL J. b. 1914 American historian. From 1969 director of the National Museum of History and Technology at the Smithsonian Institute, Washington. Author of *The Image*.

BOREISHO, MENACHEM (Goldberg) (1888–1949) Born in Brest Litovsk. Yiddish poet. Since 1914 lived in America.

BRAUDE, WILLIAM GORDON b. 1907. American Rabbi and scholar. Born Telz, Lithuania, taken to USA in 1920. Author of translation of, and critical notes on, *Pesikta Rabbati* and the *Midrash on Psalms*.

BROOKNER, ANITA b. 1928. British art historian and novelist. She won the Booker Prize for *Hotel du Lac*.

BUBER, MARTIN (1878–1965) Vienna-born, Bible-scholar and religious thinker, best known for his books on Hasidism and his philosophy of dialogue expressed in his work *I and Thou*. Settled in Palestine 1938, passionate advocate of Jewish-Arab understanding.

CANETTI, ELIAS b. 1905. Bulgarian-born novelist and essayist, of Spanish Jewish parents. Lived for many years in London while continuing to write in German. Winner of the Nobel Prize for Literature.

CHAGALL, MARC (1887–1985) Born in Vitebsk, Russia. He studied in Paris and settled in France after spending the war years in America. One of the most influential painters of this century, he produced major murals and works in stained glass. His paintings abound with biblical and Jewish imagery.

CHARLES, GERDA (Edna Lipson) Contemporary British novelist and critic.

COHEN, LEONARD b. 1934. Canadian poet, singer/songwriter and novelist.

COHEN, MARK Contemporary psychologist. Born in Scotland, settled in Israel.

COOPER, HOWARD Contemporary British Rabbi and Psychotherapist. He brings psychological insights to bear on biblical stories.

DANIEL, YULI b. 1925. Russian poet, translator and satirist. Imprisoned 1966 following notorious trial with fellow writer Andrey Sinyavsky. Released 1970, exiled from Moscow.

DUBNER MAGGID (Jacob b. Wolf Kranz. 1741–1804) Popular preacher famous for his parables.

DYLAN, BOB (Robert Zimmerman) b. 1941. American songwriter and singer. Leading figure in 1960s "protest music" scene.

EINSTEIN, ALBERT (1879–1955) German physicist, discoverer of the theory of relativity, and Nobel Prize winner. Settled in United States 1933. Ardent Zionist.

ELYASHIV, VERA b. 1929. Lithuanian political writer and journalist. Survived concentration camp and entered Palestine as illegal immigrant. Settled in London 1963.

FRANKL, VIKTOR E. b. 1905. Austrian psychiatrist. Survivor of Auschwitz. Creator of logotherapy, a therapy based on the search for meaning in life.

FREEMAN, ETHNE b. 1939. English poet.

FREUD, SIGMUND (1856–1940) Austrian psychiatrist, discoverer of the "unconscious", pioneer of psychoanalysis. Emigrated to England 1938.

FRIEDLANDER, ALBERT H. b. 1927. Reform Rabbi. Born Germany. Studied in United States. Dean of the Leo Baeck College and minister of Westminster Synagogue. Works include *Leo Baeck* and *Out of the Whirlwind*.

GARY, ROMAIN (1914–80) French novelist, born in Vilna. A fighter pilot in the French Air Force he entered the diplomatic service after the war. *Promise at Dawn*, later filmed, recounts memories of his Jewish mother.

GEBIRTIG, MORDKHE (1877–1942) Born in Cracow where he worked all his life as a carpenter. Yiddish poet and highly popular folk balladist. His song "Undzer Shtetl Brent" (Our Town is Burning), 1938, became a kind of hymn of the ghettos and concentration camps. Killed in the Cracow Ghetto.

GERSHWIN, IRA (1896–1986) American lyricist and librettist. He wrote the lyrics for music by his brother George and other composers, including Kurt Weill and Jerome Kern.

GINSBERG, ALLEN b. 1926. American poet and leader of the "Beat Generation". Draws hallucinatory pictures of alienation in contemporary America. Wrote long poem *Kaddish* after the death of his mother.

GINSBURG, NATALIA b. 1917. Italian novelist, essayist and playwright. Her first husband, a victim of the Nazis, died in a Roman prison in 1944.

GOLDBERG, LEAH (1911–70) Hebrew poet, critic, and children's writer. Born Eastern Prussia, settled in Palestine 1935.

GOLDMAN, EMMA (1869–1940) Anarchist writer, lecturer and activist. Born Lithuania, settled in the United States 1885. Fought against economic, social and sexual repression.

GOLLER, IZAK (1891–1939) British orthodox Rabbi, poet, playwright and artist. His advanced social views got him dismissed from his Liverpool congregation in 1926.

GREENBERG, FLORENCE (1882–1980) London-born cookery expert, journalist and writer.

GREENGROSS, WENDY b. 1925. British doctor, counsellor and broadcaster. Lecturer in Pastoral Care and Counselling at Leo Baeck College.

GROSSINGER, JENNIE (1892–1972) American resort owner and manager who developed a giant holiday resort in the Catskill Mountains. She prefaced her *The Art of Jewish Cooking* with her mother's words: "No one must ever go away hungry."

HAKOTUN, RABBI MOSHE. A legendary chasidic figure to whom many sayings are ascribed.

HALEVI, JUDAH (*c.* 1075–1141) Spanish Hebrew poet, philosopher and physician. Author of *The Kuzari*.

HAMMERSTEIN, OSCAR, II (1895–1960) American librettist and theatrical producer. With his partner Richard Rogers produced shows like *Oklahoma* that revolutionized the American Musical Theatre.

HANAGID, SHMUEL (Ismael Ibn Nagrel'a) (993–1055) Spanish (Granada) statesman, poet, scholar and military commander. As vizier he led the Muslim army. The Jews conferred upon him the title "Nagid" (leader) of Spanish Jewry.

HARBURG, E. Y. (Yip) (1898–1981) American songwriter. He wrote "socially conscious" songs, like "Brother, Can You Spare A Dime" during the Depression.

He created the lyrics for *The Wizard of Oz*, getting an Oscar for "Somewhere Over the Rainbow", and co-authored *Finian's Rainbow*.

HART, LORENZ (1895–1943) American songwriter. Collaborated as lyric writer with Richard Rogers in a string of successful Broadway musicals and films. Songs include "My Funny Valentine", "The Lady Is A Tramp" and "Manhattan".

HART, MOSS (1904–61) American playwright, librettist and director. He wrote satirical comedies, often with George S. Kaufmann. Directed *My Fair Lady*. His autobiography, *Act One*, is a moving account of his early life of poverty and of learning his theatrical craft.

HE-HASID, JUDAH (1150–1217) Of Regensburg. Reputed to be a mystic. Little is known of him. Associated with Sefer Chasidim.

HEIMLER, EUGENE b. 1922. Poet, writer and psychiatric social worker. Born Hungary, settled in England 1947 after surviving Auschwitz. The camp experiences are recalled in *Night of the Mist*, his subsequent recovery in *A Link in the Chain*. Professor of Human Social Functioning at the University of Calgary in Canada.

HEINE, HEINRICH (1797–1856) German poet and essayist. Converted to Christianity 1825, but retained a strong Jewish identity. Exiled in France. Prophetic insight into the later course of German history.

HELLER, BUNAM b. 1908. Yiddish poet and ardent Communist. Disillusioned after the liquidation of the Jewish Anti-Fascist Committee in 1948. Born Warsaw, emigrated to Israel 1957.

HELLMAN, LILLIAN (1905–84) American writer and playwright. Author of the play *The Little Foxes* and collections of memoirs, including *Pentimento*.

HESCHEL, ABRAHAM JOSHUA (1907–72) American Conservative Rabbi, scholar and theologian. Professor of Jewish Ethics and Mysticism at the Jewish Theological Seminary of America. Author of *God in Search of Man*.

HILLEL. First century teacher. Born in Babylon, became a leading authority in Jerusalem on the interpretation of Jewish law. Renowned for his humanity and ethical teachings, for his formulation of the Golden Rule and the leniency of his legal decisions.

HINDUS, MILTON Contemporary American scholar, literary critic and educator. Professor of Humanities at Brandeis University.

HOLTZ, BARRY Contemporary American poet and essayist.

IBN GABIRQL, SOLOMON (1021–56) Spanish poet and neo-Platonic philosopher. His major work, *Mekor Hayyim* (*The Source of Life*), was preserved in a Latin version, *Fons Vitae*. Author of the philosophical poem *Keter Malkhut* (The Kingly Crown), read in Sephardi tradition on the night or dawn on *Yom Kippur*.

IBN PAKUDA, BACHYA (*c.* 1050–1120) Religious philosopher. His *Duties of the Heart* speaks of trust in God, humility, and asceticism. Strong affinity with Arab mystics.

IBN VERGA, SOLOMON (Fifteenth–sixteenth centuries) Historian and Marrano. Wrote on persecution and disputation (*Rod of Judah*).

JACOBS, ARTHUR b. 1937. Scottish poet and translator.

KAFKA, FRANZ (1883–1924) Czech novelist whose works express the confusion and loss of identity felt by Western man. His works include *The Trial* and *Metamorphosis*.

KAPLAN, HAYYIM A. (1880–?1942) Russian-born teacher and educator. Kept an eye-witness account of the Nazi occupation of Warsaw from 1st September 1939 till August 1942. Found twenty years later, this diary was published as *Scroll of Agony*.

KINDERLEHRER, JANE Contemporary American cookery writer and nutritionist. Senior editor of *Prevention*, a magazine for nutrition and good health.

KLEIN, ABRAHAM MOSES (1909–1972) Canadian poet and author. Born in Montreal, a partner in a law firm, he was a creative and influential poet exploring Jewish and Canadian themes.

KLEPFISZ, IRENA Born 1941 in Warsaw. Emigrated to America in 1949. A lecturer in Yiddish and Women's Studies, her fiction, poetry and essays deal with Jewish and feminist themes.

KOESTLER, ARTHUR (1905–83) Hungarian-born journalist, novelist and intellectual. Explored the social, political and scientific issues of our time.

KOOK, ABRAHAM ISAAC (RAV KOOK) (1865–1935) First Ashkenazi Chief Rabbi of Palestine. Born Latvia. Concerned with the religious problems of the new settlement. Combined ardent Zionism with deep mysticism.

KOPP, SHELDON Contemporary American psychotherapist.

KOSOV, NACHMAN OF (d. 1746) Kabbalist and one of the early Chasidim – a contemporary of the Besht. He emphasized devotion in prayer and constant contemplation of God.

KOSSOFF, DAVID b. 1919. British actor and broadcaster, particularly well-known for adapting Bible stories for children.

LANDAU, ZISHA (1889–1937) Yiddish poet, playwright and translator. Born Poland, settled United States 1906. Affected by Jewish suffering in World War I, he wrote on Jewish national themes.

LEKHIVITZER, NOAH (d. 1833) Chasidic Rabbi.

LEVIN, BERNARD b. 1928. British critic and journalist.

LEWISOHN, LUDWIG (1882–1955) American translator, novelist and essayist. Born in Germany, his pacifism lost him his academic post during World War I and he spent the interwar years in Paris. Discovering his Jewish roots he became a strong advocate of Zionism.

LIPPMANN, WALTER (1889–1974) American journalist, editor and political philosopher.

LUCAS, ALICE (1852–1935) British poet and translator of medieval liturgical poetry.

LUTZKY, A. (Aaron Zuker) (1893–1957) Russian-born Yiddish poet. Settled in New York in 1914.

MACCOBY, HYAM ZOUNDELL b. 1924. Scholar, author and playwright. Librarian of Leo Baeck College. Writer on different aspects of Jewish-Christian Relations and the origins of anti-semitism. His book *The Day God Laughed* illustrates Jewish wit and humour in early Rabbinic sources.

MAGONET, JONATHAN b. 1942. British Reform Rabbi, doctor, and Principal of the Leo Baeck College. Co-editor of the Daily and Sabbath Prayer Book, and the High Holy Day Prayer Book of the reform synagogues of Great Britain. Editor of *Returning*.

MAIMONIDES, MOSES (RAMBAM) (1135–1204) Philosopher, halakhist and physician. Born Spain, settled in Cairo *c.* 1166. Wrote *Mishneh Torah* and *Guide for the Perplexed*. One of the greatest Jewish legal authorities of all time.

MALAMUD, BERNARD (1914–87) American novelist. His novel *The Fixer*, telling of a Jew falsely accused of committing ritual murder in Russia, is a powerful study of human courage. It won the Pulitzer Prize for Literature.

MARX, HARPO (Adolph/Arthur) (1893–1964) American vaudeville and film comedian, the "silent" member of the Marx Brothers. His autobiography is called *Harpo Speaks*.

MARX, KARL HEINRICH (1818–83) German social philosopher. Born of baptized Jewish parents, settled in England 1852. Chief theorist of modern socialism.

MAYBAUM, IGNAZ (1897–1976) Reform Rabbi and theologian. Born in Vienna, settled in England 1939. His books include *The Face of God after Auschwitz*, and *Trialogue*, an exploration of Jewish-Christian-Muslim relations. First teacher of Theology at Leo Baeck College.

MENASHE, SAMUEL Contemporary poet. The quotation from his mother, Sarah Brana Barak, appears in his collection *Fringe of Fire*.

MILEJKOWSKI, ISRAEL (d. 1943) Polish doctor, responsible for public health in the Warsaw Ghetto. To show the world the crippling effects of starvation imposed by the Nazis on the Ghetto he organized the doctors to document their findings – republished in 1979 as *Hunger Disease*. He died at his own hand.

MILLER, ARTHUR b. 1915. American playwright and novelist. His play *Death of a Salesman* won the Pulitzer Prize. His works explore social issues and his concern with freedom of conscience.

MOLODOVSKY, KADIA b. 1894. Yiddish poet and novelist. Born Lithuania, settled in New York 1935.

NACHMAN OF BRATSLAV (1772–1811) Chasidic rabbi and ascetic. Used stories and parables to illustrate his mystical theology. Great grandson of the Baal Shem Tov.

NEMEROV, HOWARD b. 1920. American poet and novelist.

NEUBERGER, JULIA b. 1950. British Liberal Rabbi, broadcaster, political activist and writer.

NEWMAN, JEFFREY b. 1941. British Reform Rabbi. Graduate of Leo Baeck College.

NIKNAM, MARY (Begej) Contemporary. Born in Persia, settled in Britain where she works as an interpreter.

OMER-MAN, JONATHAN (Derek Orlans) British-born writer and religious counsellor. Edited *Shefa*, a magazine of Jewish thought, in Jerusalem. Now lives in America.

PARKER, DOROTHY (1893–1967) American poet and author. She built a reputation as a critic and a wit. There is a deep seriousness beneath the light surface of much of her work.

PENINI, YEDAYA Poet and philosopher. Lived in Provence late fourteenth and early fifteenth century.

PETUCHOWSKI, JAKOB JOSEPH b. 1925. Reform Rabbi, scholar and theologian. Born Berlin, emigrated to England 1939, settled in United States 1949. Professor of Rabbinics at Hebrew Union College. His writings include several works on liturgy. Author of *Prayer Book Reform in Europe*.

PHILO (*c.* 20 BCE–CE 50) Jewish philosopher living in Alexandria, who sought to harmonize Greek philosophy with Judaism.

PRAWER-JHABVALA, RUTH. Born in Germany of Polish parents. Lives in India. Writer of short stories, novels and screenplays, including *Shakespeare Wallah* and *Heat and Dust*.

PROUST, MARCEL (1871–1922) French novelist. His major work *A la Recherche du Temps Perdu* (Remembrance of Things Past) (fifteen volumes – 1913–1927) reflects in part the conflicts between his (maternal) Jewish and non-Jewish heritage.

RASHI (Rabbi Solomon ben Isaac) (1040–1105) French Rabbi and leading scholar of his age. His commentary accompanied the first printed edition of the Hebrew Bible. His *Talmud* commentary is still considered the standard tool for its study.

RAVAGE, MARCUS Contemporary American essayist.

REISEN, ABRAHAM (1876–1953) Russian. One of the most popular Yiddish writers and poets. Settled in America 1908.

REZNIKOFF, CHARLES (1894–1976) American lawyer and poet. Selected edition of his poems published as *By the Waters of Manhattan*.

RICH, ADRIENNE Contemporary American poet and essayist. Involved in civil rights and feminist issues.

ROLNIK, JOSEPH (1879–1955) Yiddish poet. Born Russia, settled in United States 1908. Living in New York, his later poems recalled the Lithuanian villages of his childhood.

ROSENZWEIG, FRANZ (1886–1929) German philosopher and Jewish educator. The deep impression made by a Yom Kippur service prevented his intended conversion to Christianity. Author of *Star of Redemption* and co-translator of the Bible into German with Buber.

ROTH, LEON (1896–1963) English-born philosopher and educator;

professor at Hebrew University 1928–53. Gave the address at the opening of the Leo Baeck College.

RUDIN, JACOB PHILIP b. 1902. American Reform Rabbi.

SACHS, NELLY (1891–1970) German playwright and poet. Nobel prize winner. Her reputation is based on her poetic response to the Holocaust.

SCHALOM ALEICHEM (Shalom Rabinowitz) (1859–1916) Born in the Ukraine. Yiddish author and humorist. His monologues about Tevya the Milkman were the basis of the musical *Fiddler on the Roof*.

SCHIFF, HILDA Contemporary British writer and poet.

SCHNITZLER, ARTHUR (1862–1931) Austrian playwright and author. A doctor of medicine, interested in psychotherapy, his writings explored human relationships and anti-semitism. His play *Reigen* became internationally known through the film version *La Ronde*.

SCHOLEM, GERSHOM (1897–1981) German-born scholar of Jewish mysticism, who created and established this field of study. From 1923 taught at the Hebrew University in Jerusalem.

SCHWARZ, EDNA Contemporary American poet and translator of Spanish Jewish poetry.

SENESH, HANNAH (1921–44) Born Hungary, settled Palestine 1939. Volunteered for rescue mission and parachuted back into Hungary, where captured and shot. Some of her poems were set to music.

SHIMMEL, MOSHE Born 1904 in Lemberg. Polish poet, turned to writing in Yiddish.

SIMON, PAUL b. 1941. American songwriter and performer.

SINGER, ISAAC BASHEVIS Born 1904 in Radzymin, Poland, lives in New York. Yiddish story writer, novelist and journalist. Nobel Prize for Literature in 1978.

SMITH, DANIEL Contemporary British Reform Rabbi, graduate of Leo Baeck College.

SOTTO-BOLGAR, ANNA Contemporary poet. Resident in Israel.

STEIN, GERTRUDE (1874–1946) American author, critic and patron of the arts. Her "salon" in Paris became a centre of artistic life.

STEINBERG, MILTON (1903–50) American Conservative Rabbi. His books include *Basic Judaism*.

TUBY, MOLLY Born in Egypt, settled in Britain. Leading Analytical Psychologist.

TUSSMAN, MALKA HEIFETZ b. 1896. Yiddish poet and translator. Born Ukraine, settled in United States in 1912.

TUWIM, JULJAN (1894–1953) Polish poet and satirist. Returned to Poland after the Second World War.

VOGEL, DAVID (1891–1943) Russian-born poet and novelist who wrote in Hebrew. He lived in Palestine and Europe, died in a concentration camp.

WALD, LILLIAN (1867–1940) United States social worker and campaigner for social reforms.

WEIL, SIMONE (1909–43) French philosopher and mystic. Lived a life of voluntary hardship and deprivation in the style of medieval Christian mystics, but never formally converted to Christianity. Joined the Free French forces in London where she died. Books include *Waiting on God*.

WEISS, JOSEPH (1918–69) Born Hungary, settled in Great Britain. Scholar of the history of Chasidism. Professor of Jewish Studies at the University of London.

WIESEL, ELIE b. 1928. Writer. Born in Transylvania and interned in Auschwitz and Buchenwald. His books concentrate on Jewish themes, his wartime experiences and Chasidism. Nobel Peace Prize.

WOLFSKEHL, KARL (1869–1948) German poet. Left Germany 1934, settled in New Zealand 1938. He felt a deep commitment to Germany, tracing his ancestry there for several centuries. His poems in exile reflect his deep sense of loss.

WOUK, HERMAN b. 1915. American novelist and playwright. Works include *The Caine Mutiny* and *This is My God*.

YEHOASH (Solomon Bloomgarten) (1872–1927) Yiddish poet and Bible translator. Born Lithuania, lived in United States and Palestine. Translated Bible into Yiddish.

YELLEN, JACK b. 1892. American songwriter. Songs include "Ain't She Sweet" and "Happy Days are Here Again".

ZEITLIN, HILLEL (1871–1942) Russian writer, thinker and journalist. He returned to religion and became deeply absorbed in mysticism. Died a martyr's death on the way to Treblinka.

ZELDA (Zelda Mishkovsky) (1914 –84) Hebrew poetess. Born Ukraine, settled in Palestine in 1925. Deep religious beliefs are expressed in her poetry.

ZWEIG, STEFAN (1881–1942) Austrian biographer, essayist, playwright and poet. As a refugee from the Nazis, he died in Rio de Janeiro in a suicide pact with his wife.

What's What

ADAR. Twelfth month of the Jewish calendar (February/March).

AGGADAH. Rabbinic teaching of homilectical character – parables, wise sayings, etc. As distinct from legal material (HALAKHAH).

ASHKENAZI. Jews originating from Central or Eastern Europe.

AZAZEL. The name of the place to which one of the goats in the Temple service on Yom Kippur was sent as an atonement for the sins of Israel.

BABA METZIA (Middle Section). Tractate in the Mishnah and in the Talmud in order Nezikin (Damages). Deals with laws of lost property, business transactions and employment.

BERACHOT. First tractate of the Mishnah, order Zeraim (Seeds). Deals with the recitation of the Shema and blessings and prayers in general.

CHAROSETH. Mixture of chopped nuts, apple, cinnamon and wine used with bitter herbs on the Passover night. It symbolizes the mortar used by the Israelites when they were slaves in Egypt.

CHASIDISM (Hasidism). (See also Baal Shem Tov.) A religious and social movement which developed quickly in depressed Eastern Europe following the Chmielnicki massacre and persecution. It has parallels with other popular religious movements of the same period.

ECCLESIASTES RABBAH. See Midrash Rabbah.

ERUBIN. Second tractate of the Mishnah, order Moed (Seasons), dealing with restrictions on carrying, walking, and cooking on Sabbath and festivals.

EXODUS RABBAH. See Midrash Rabbah.

GENESIS RABBAH. Midrashic commentary to the Book of Genesis. See Midrash Rabbah.

HALAKHAH (Pathway). Jewish law, covering all aspects of life, derived from the Torah and developed through the interpretation of the Rabbis.

HAMANTASCHEN (Haman's ears). Triangular-shaped cake filled with poppy-seed or prunes, eaten at the feast of *Purim*.

HANUKKAH. Eight-day winter festival commemorating the successful Maccabean revolt against Hellenizing Syrians (2nd Century BCE).

HASIDISM (see CHASIDISM).

HIGH HOLYDAYS. The period of the Jewish New Year comprising:

Rosh Hashanah, New Year's Day; *Yom Kippur,* the Day of Atonement and the intervening "Ten Days of Penitence" (September/October).

KABBALAH. ("Reception"). Jewish mystical tradition. (See ZOHAR).

KADDISH. Aramaic prayer at the conclusion of public services and of sections within it. Often recited as a memorial to the dead, it is in fact a messianic prayer in praise of life and God's greatness.

KASHA. Buckwheat groats.

KITZUR SHULCHAN ARUCH. Simplified edition of the *Shulchan Aruch* by Solomon Ganzfried (1804–86).

KNAIDLACH (Matzo Balls). Small dumplings eaten in soup. Often made at Passover.

KNISHES. Hot, savoury-filled, pastry snacks.

KUGEL. Yiddish term for "pudding".

LEVITICUS RABBAH. Midrashic commentary on the Book of Leviticus. See *Midrash Rabbah.*

MACHZOR (Cycle). Prayer Book for the Jewish festivals.

MAKKOT (Stripes). Fifth tractate of the Mishnah, order Nezikin (Damages), dealing with punishments administered by the court, false witnesses and cities of refuge.

MARRANO. Spanish word: "Swine". Applied in Spain and Portugal to descendants of baptized Jews suspected of secret adherence to Judaism. Victims of the Inquisition.

MEGILLAH (Scroll). Tenth tractate of the Mishnah, order Moed (Seasons) dealing with the reading of the Book of Esther on the feast of *Purim.*

MIDRASH. The finding of new meaning, in addition to the literal one, of biblical texts. Sometimes midrash teaches law (*halakhah*), at other times myths, legends, ethics, parables, etc. (*aggadah*).

MIDRASH RABBAH. A collection of midrashim on the Pentateuch and the five Megillot (Scrolls). The books stem from different periods and differ among themselves in their general character.

MIDRASH PSALMS. A midrashic collection on the Psalms.

MIKVEH. Ritual bath.

MISHNAH. Legal codification of the Oral Law, compiled by Rabbi Judah HaNasi, second century. It is divided into six orders – (*a*) *Zeraim* (seeds) dealing primarily with agricultural laws, but also containing the rules of prayer; (*b*) *Moed* (Seasons) dealing with the Sabbath, Festivals, etc.; (*c*) *Nashim* (Women) dealing with marriage and divorce and vows; (*d*) *Nezikin* (Damages) dealing with civil and criminal legislation; (*e*) *Kodashim* (Holy things) dealing with the laws of slaughter, sacrifice, and consecrated objects; (*f*) *Taharot* (Purities) dealing with laws of ritual purity. Each order is then subdivided, forming a total of 63 tractates, which are then further treated in the Gemara. Mishnah and Gemara together make up the Talmud.

MITZVAH "Commandment" or "precept". A legal or social obligation incumbent on all Jews. From this it acquires the more general meaning of "good deed".

NEILAH (Closing). Concluding service of *Yom Kippur*, whose name derives from the closing of the gates of heaven that had been open to receive the prayers of worshippers.

NUMBERS RABBAH. Midrashic commentary to the Book of Numbers. See *Midrash Rabbah*.

PAREVE (pronounced "parveh") ("neutral food"). A term for foods that are neither meat nor milk (which must be kept separate in Jewish tradition) and so can be eaten with either.

PASSOVER. First of the three Pilgrim Festivals celebrated annually by Jews. It commemorates the exodus from Egypt.

PESACHIM (Passover). Tractate in the Mishnah and in the Talmud in order Mo'ed (Seasons). Deals with the laws of Passover.

PESIKTA D' RAV KAHANA. Collection of Midrashim on the Festivals and special Sabbaths of the year; probably fifth century.

PESIKTA RABBATI. Collection of Midrashim on the Festivals and special Sabbaths of the year; probably seventh century.

PHYLACTERIES (Heb. *Tefillin*). Small black leather boxes containing Bible verses and attached to black leather straps, which adults wear during prayer at weekday morning services.

PIRKEI AVOT. – See SAYINGS OF THE FATHERS.

ROSH HASHANAH (lit "Head (i.e. "Beginning") of the Year"). (*a*) The birthday of the world in Jewish tradition on which it is judged by God. (*b*) Eighth trac-

tate in the Mishnah, order Moed (Seasons) dealing with the New Year.

SANHEDRIN. Fourth tractate of the Mishnah, order Nezikin (damages), dealing with courts of justice and judicial procedures, particularly criminal law and punishments.

SAYINGS OF THE FATHERS (*Pirkei Avot*). Tractate of the Mishnah with no talmudic commentary. Contains sayings of Rabbis and teachers from the third century BCE to the third century CE. It is read in Ashkenazi communities on Sabbath afternoons.

SEFER CHASIDIM (Book of the Pious). Ethical teachings of the *Chasidei Ashkenaz*, a German mystical movement of the twelfth and early thirteenth centuries.

SEFER TORAH. Handwritten parchment scroll containing the Five Books of Moses. Kept in the Ark of the Synagogue and read on Sabbaths, certain weekdays and at Festivals.

SHOFAR. Musical instrument made from an animal's (generally ram's) horn, blown on the High Holy Days and during the preceding month to awake people to repentance.

SHULHAN ARUKH (The Prepared Table). Authoritative code of Jewish law and practice written by Joseph Caro (1488–1575); published Venice 1565.

SIDDUR ("Arrangement", "order"). The Jewish prayerbook in which liturgical texts are arranged in a set "order".

SOTAH. Fifth tractate in the Mishnah, order Nashim (Women)

WHAT'S WHAT · 221

dealing with the woman suspected of adultery (Numbers 5:12–31).

SUCCAH (Booth). Tractate in the Mishnah and in the Talmud in order *Moed* (Seasons). Deals with the festival of *Succot* (Booths, Tabernacles), which commemorates the wandering of the Israelites in the wilderness.

TA'ANIT (Fast). Tractate in the Mishnah and in the Talmud in order Moed (Seasons). Deals with the special fasts (e.g. at times of drought).

TALMUD (Teaching). Compilation of the commentaries of the Rabbis on the Mishnah from 2nd –5th centuries, covering both religious and civil matters. A mixture of laws, customs, discussions, stories and *obiter dicta*, it became the foundation of Jewish practice throughout the world. Two versions; one compiled in Palestine (the *Yerushalmi*) completed about 400 CE; the other in Babylon (the *Bavli*) completed between 100–300 years later, the latter being authoritative.

TEIGLACH. Round dough cakes cooked in honey.

TOBIT. One of the books of the Apocrypha.

TORAH (Teaching). The Five Books of Moses (Pentateuch). The term is also used to mean the whole of the Bible and subsequent Jewish teaching.

UNETANNEH TOKEF (We declare how profound . . .). Opening words of *piyyut* (liturgical poem) for *Rosh Hashanah* and *Yom Kippur* which emphasizes the Day of Judgement. Ascribed to Kalonymus ben Meshullam ben Kalonymus (eleventh century). Associated in legend with martyred Rabbi Amnon of Mainz.

YAHRZEIT. Yiddish term meaning the anniversary of a close relative's death. Lit. "year's time".

YESHIVAH (lit. "session", "a sitting"). A college of traditional Jewish learning, specifically designed for the study of Talmud.

YIDDISH. A language derived principally from Middle High German and Hebrew, written in Hebrew characters. It assimilated elements from the various countries in which it was the *lingua franca* of the Jewish population, principally Eastern Europe.

YOM KIPPUR (Day of Atonement). The tenth day of the Jewish New Year, the most solemn occasion of the Jewish Calendar. A day of fasting and prayer which climaxes the penitential season.

ZADDIK. Lit. "The righteous one". Leader of a Chasidic community.

ZAFTIG. Yiddish term equivalent to "pleasingly plump".

ZOHAR (Splendour). Major work of *kaballah* (Jewish mysticism), an esoteric commentary on the Torah. Compiled and edited by Moses ben Shem Tov Leon in thirteenth century, although traditionally ascribed to second-century Shimon bar Yohai.

Acknowledgements

The authors and publishers are grateful for permission to use the following material.

Israel Abrahams, *Festival Studies*, Macmillan Publishing Co. (1906)

H. Arendt, "The Human Condition", University of Chicago (1958)

Rose Ausländer, "The Foreigners", Deutscher Taschenbuch Verlag and "Accusation" (source unknown)

Nathan Ausubel Ed., *A Treasury of Jewish Humour*, Doubleday (1955)
A Treasury of Jewish Folklore, Crown Publishers

Leo Baeck, *The Essence of Judaism*, Schocken Books (1961)

J. L. Baron Ed., *Treasury of Jewish Quotations*, Thomas Yosleoff (1965)

Isaac Bashevis Singer, Nobel Lecture (1978) Jonathan Cape Ltd.
First published by Farrar, Straus & Giroux Ltd

Menachem Begin, *White Nights: the story of a prisoner in Russia* (Steimatzky Ltd ©)

Saul Bellow, *Herzog*, Penguin (1964)

Bernard Berenson, "November 7, 1953 aged 89" from *The Diaries of 1947–1958*, Ed. Nicky Mariano, Hamish Hamilton (1964)

Alexander Bergman, *A Treasury of Jewish Poetry*, Crown Publishers (1957)

Lionel Blue and June Rose, *A Taste of Heaven*, published 1977 by Darton Longman and Todd and used by permission of the publishers

Daniel Boorstin, *The Image*, Atheneum Publishers (1963)

William G. Brande, "What I learned in Alabama about Yarmultes" (1965)

Anita Brookner, *A Start In Life*, Jonathan Cape Ltd (1981)

Lewis Browne, *The Wisdom of Israel*, Michael Joseph (1958)

Martin Buber, *Ten Rungs: Hasidic Sayings* (1962) and *Tales of the Hasidim* (1961) Schocken Books

Martin Buber, *The Way of Man*, Routledge & Kegan Paul (1963)

Theodore L. Bross Ed., *The Literature of the Jews*, Macmillan Publishing Co.

Elias Canetti, *The Human Province*, André Deutsch Ltd (1986)
The Voices of Marrakech, Marion Boyars Publishers (1978)
Marc Chagall, *Marc Chagall*, Thames and Hudson Ltd (1966)
Gerda Charles, "Is There Life After Death?", printed in the *Jewish Chronicle* (4 February 1983)
L. Cohen, "Adolph Eichmann" from *Flowers for Hitler*. Used by permission of the Canadian Publishers, McCellend and Stewart, Toronto
Howard Cooper (source untraced)
Yuli Daniel, *Prison Poems* translated by David Bury and Arthur Boyars, Marion Boyars Publishers (1971)
Bob Dylan, *Writings and Drawings* (1973)
Viktor E. Frankl, *Man's Search for Meaning*, Hodder & Stoughton
Ethne Freeman (source untraced)
Albert H. Friedlander, "Thought for the Day"
Solomon Ganzfried, *Code of Jewish Law* translated by Harry E. Goldin, Star Hebrew Publishing Co. (1927)
Romain Gary, *Promise at Dawn: A Memoir*, Harper & Row (1961)
Mordkhe Gebirtig, "Yankele" from *The Shtetl Book*, Ed. Diane K. Roskies and Daniel G. Roskies, Ktav Publishing House (1975)
Ira Gershwin, *Lyrics on Several Occasions*, Hamish Hamilton (1978)
Allen Ginsberg, *Kaddish and other Poems*, City Light Books (1961)
Natalia Ginsberg, *Never must you ask me*, Michael Joseph (1973)
Nakum Glatzer Ed., *Language of Faith*, Schocken Books (1947).
A Jewish Reader, Schocken Books (1961)
Leah Goldberg, "The Eighth Part (at least) of everything" from *Selected Poems by Leah Goldberg*, translated by Robert Friend, Menard/Panjandrum (1976) © Robert Friend
Emma Goldman, *Living My Life*, The New American Library (1977)
Isak Goller, "The Pious Men of –", *The Passionate Jew*, The Merton Press (1923)
Florence Greenberg, "Charoseth", *Jewish Cookery*, Hamlyn Publishing Group
Rabbi Sidney Greenberg, *A Treasury of Comfort*, Prayer Book Press
Jenny Grossinger, "Potato Kugel", *The Art of Jewish Cooking*, Bantam Press (1964)
Frederic V. Grunfeld, *Prophets Without Honour*, Hutchinson Publishing Group (1979)
Moshe Haktun, *God of a Hundred Names*, Victor Gollancz
Judah Halevi, *Selected Poems of Judah Halevi*, Jewish Publication Society of America (1924)
Oscar Hammerstein II, "Ol' Man River", composer Jerome Kern, © 1927 T. B. Harms Co. Used by permission of Chappell Music Ltd
E. Y. Harburg, "Somewhere Over The Rainbow" from *The Wizard of Oz*

(1939). "Brother Can You Spare A Dime?", composer Jay Gorney © 1932 Harms Inc. Used by permission of Chappell Music Ltd

Lorenz Hart, "Ten Cents A Dance", composer Richard Rogers, © 1930 Harms Inc. Used by permission of Chappell Music Ltd

Moss Hart, *Act One: An Autobiography*, Random House, Inc.

Eugene Heimler, *Night of Mist* (1959), *A Link in the Chain*

Heinrich Heine, "A Childhood Conception" translated by H. Walter, and "My Child, we two were children" translated by Alma Strettel, from *Heine: Prose and Poetry*, Everyman's Library volume, J. M. Dent & Sons Ltd (1934)

Heinrich Heine "Absolutely" (source untraced)

Lillian Hellman, *Scoundrel Time*, Macmillan Publishing Co. (1976)

A. J. Heschel, "To Grow in Wisdom" printed in *Judaism* (Spring 1977) *Man is Not Alone*, Harper & Row (1951)

Milton Hindus, "The Army of The Dead" from *The Broken Music Box*, The Menard Press (1980)

Barry Holtz, "Yahrzeit Poem" published in *Response* (Summer 1974)

Irving Howe, *The Immigrant Jews of New York*, Routledge & Kegan Paul (1976)

A. C. Jacobs, "Where" from *The Proper Blessing*, The Menard Press (1976)

Franz Kafka, *Parables and Paradoxes* (1946). "19 October 1921" from *Franz Kafka Diaries* (1949)

John Keats, *You Might As Well Live*, Martin Secker & Warburg Ltd (1975)

Jane Kinderlehrer, "Adding Nutrition to Tradition", from *Cooking Kosher The Natural Way*, Jonathan David Publishers Inc., 68–22 Eliot Avenue, Middle Village, NY11379

Francine Klagsbrum, *Voices of Wisdom*, Random House (1980)

Irena Klepfisz, "Bashert", *Keeper of Accounts*

Franz Kobler Ed., *Letters of the Jews Throughout the Ages*, Ararat Publishing Society Ltd (1952)

Arthur Koestler, *Dialogue with Death*, Hutchinson Publishing Group (1961) Reprinted by permission of A. D. Peters & Co. Ltd

Sheldon Kopp, *If You Meet the Buddha on the Road, Kill Him*, Bantam Books (1980)

Simon G. Kramer, *God and Man in the Sefer Hasidim*, Bloch Publishing Co. (1966)

A. I. Ktah Ed., *The Warsaw Diary of Chaim A. Kaplan*, Hamish Hamilton (1966)

Zishe Landau "Tonight", translated by Edward Field, from *A Treasury of Yiddish Poetry* edited by Irving Howe and Eliezer Greenberg. Reprinted by permission of Henry Holt and Company, Inc.

J. Leftwich Ed., *The Way We Think: A Collection of Essays from the Yiddish*, *Vol. II*, Thomas Yoseloff (1969)

Bernard Levin, *Conducted Tour*, Jonathan Cape Ltd (1981)

Alice Lucas, *The Jewish Year* (source untraced)

A. Lutzky, *The Golden Peacock*, Ed. Joseph Leftwich, Robert Anscombe Ltd (1939)

Hyam Maccoby, *The Day That God Laughed*, Robson Books

Harpo Marx, *Harpo Speaks*, Robson Books

Ignaz Maybaum, *The Faith of the Jewish Diaspora*, Vision Press. *Creation and Guilt* (1969)

Samuel Menashe, *Fringe of Fire: Poems of Samuel Menashe*, Victor Gollancz

Dr Alter B. Z. Metzger, *Lights of Return: Rabbi Kook's Philosophy of Repentance*, Yeshiva University (1978)

Midstream Vol. 25 No. 5 (May 1979)

Arthur Miller, *Death of a Salesman*, Penguin Books Ltd (1961). © Arthur Miller 1949.

Kadia Molodovsky, "A Poem of Women" from *A Jewish Liberation Anthology*, New Glide Publications (1977)

Louis I. Newman, *Hasidic Anthology* (1963)

J. Newman (source untraced)

Simon Novlek, "Milton Steinberg's Philosophy of Religion", printed in *Judaism* (Winter 1977)

Jonathan Omer-Man, New Traditions (Spring 1984), National Hauurah Committee

Dorothy Parker, *The Portable Dorothy Parker*, Viking Press

W. Gunther Plaut Ed., "Der Morgen", German Jewish Journal before World War II; translated and reprinted in W. Gunter Plaut's *The Growth of Reform Judaism New York*; World Union of Progressive Judaism (1965) pp. 135–6

Ruth Prawer Jhabvala, "Myself in India" from *How I Became A Holy Mother*, John Murray (Publishers) Ltd

Charles Reznikoff, *Poems 1937–1975, Vol. II*, Black Sparrow Press (1977)

Adrienne Rich, *On Lies, Secrets and Silence: Selected Prose 1966–1978*, 1979 by W. W. Norton & Company, Inc. First published in America by W. W. Norton & Company, Inc. 1979. Published by Virago Press 1980

Franz Rosenweig, *The Star of Redemption*, Routledge & Kegan Paul (1971)

Leon Roth, *God and Man in the Old Testament*, Unwin Hyman Ltd (1955)

Ruth Rubin Ed., "Bulbes" from *Jewish Folk Songs in Yiddish and English*, translated by Ruth Rubin, Appleseed Music Inc. (1964)

Ruth Rubin, *Voices of a People* (1963)

Nelly Sachs, "To you that Build the New House", translated by Michael Hamburger, Jonathan Cape Ltd

Gershom Schalem, *Major Trends in Jewish Mysticism*, Thames and Hudson Ltd (1955)

Hilda Schiff, "To My Mother" published in *Translantic Review* (Autumn 1966)

Howard Schwartz and Anthony Rudolf Ed., The Menard Press. "Waiting Rooms" from *Anthology of Modern Hebrew Poetry* selected by S. Y. Penueli and A. Ukhmani, Israel Universities Press (1966)

Paul Simon, "One Trick Pony", Pattern Music Ltd (1979)

Anna Sotto, "Only Me". Published in *Voices, Israel*, Vol. II (1983)

David Vogel, "When I was Growing Up . . ." from *The Dark Gate, Selected Poems of David Vogel*, translated by A. C. Jacobs, the Menard Press 1976. © Arthur Jacobs

Elie Wiesel, *The Gates of Forest*, Heinemann (1967)

Myron Winick Ed., *Hunger Studies by the Jewish Physicians in the Warsaw Ghettos*, John Wiley & Sons (1979)

Herman Wouk, *This Is My God*, The Abe Wouk Foundation (1959)

Jack Yellen, "My Yiddish Momma" from *Sophie Tucker: Some of These Days*, © 1925 De Sylva Brown. Henderson Inc., subsequently published by EMI Music Publishers Ltd, London WC2H 0LD. Reproduced by permission of EMI Music Publishers Ltd and International Music Publications

Jack Yellen, "Life Begins at Forty" from *Sophie Tucker: Some of These Days*, © Jack Yellen and Shapiro 1937. Reproduced by permission of International Music Publications

Zelda, "L'Chrish Yesh Shem" from the *Collection Paray*, translated by Jonathan Magonet, Hakibtutz Hamenchad Publishing House Ltd

Stephen Zweig, *The World of Yesteryear*, originally published by Cassell in 1943 and reprinted by them in 1987

Forms of Prayer, Vol. I (Siddur): Daily and Sabbath Prayers, published by Reform Synagogues of Great Britain

Forms of Prayer, Vol. III (Machzor): Days of Awe: Prayers for the High Holy Days, published by Reform Synagogues of Great Britain